Service as the
Path of a
Meaningful Life

Stick Your Neck Out

A Street-Smart
Guide to Creating
Change in
Your Community
and Beyond

JOHN GRAHAM

President of the Giraffe Heroes Project

BK

BERRETT-KOEHLER PUBLISHERS, INC.
San Francisco

Berrett-Koehler Publishers, Inc.
235 Montgomery Street, Suite 650
San Francisco, CA 94104-2916
Tel: (415) 288-0260   Fax: (415) 362-2512   www.bkconnection.com

Ordering Information

Quantity sales. Special discounts are available on quantity purchases by
corporations, associations, and others. For details, contact the "Special Sales
Department" at the Berrett-Koehler address above.

Individual sales. Berrett-Koehler publications are available through most
bookstores. They can also be ordered directly from Berrett-Koehler: Tel: (800)
929-2929; Fax: (802) 864-7626; www.bkconnection.com.

Orders for college textbook/course adoption use.
Please contact Berrett-Koehler: Tel: (800) 929-2929; Fax: (802) 864-7626.

Orders by U.S. trade bookstores and wholesalers.
Please contact Publishers Group West, 1700 Fourth Street, Berkeley, CA 94710.
Tel: (510) 528-1444; Fax (510) 528-3444.

Berrett-Koehler and the BK logo are registered trademarks of
Berrett-Koehler Publishers, Inc.

Printed in the United States of America

Berrett-Koehler books are printed on long-lasting acid-free paper. When it is
available, we choose paper that has been manufactured by environmentally
responsible processes. These may include using trees grown in sustainable
forests, incorporating recycled paper, minimizing chlorine in bleaching, or
recycling the energy produced at the paper mill.

Library of Congress Cataloging-in-Publication Data
Graham, John, 1942–
Stick your neck out : a street-smart guide to creating change in your community
and beyond : service as the path of a meaningful life / by John Graham.
p. cm.
Includes bibliographical reference and index.
ISBN–13: 978-1-57675-304-0
1. Social action—Handbooks, manuals, etc.
2. Social change—Citizen participation—Handbooks, manuals, etc.
3. Community power—Handbooks, manuals, etc.
I. Title.
HN18.G665 2005
307.1'4—dc22   2004062708

First Edition
10 09 08 07 06 05   10 9 8 7 6 5 4 3 2 1

CONTENTS

CHAPTER TWO

START HERE 17

Research
Decide the Form of Your Participation
Create a Specific Project
Create a Vision for Your Project's Success
Add Details to Your Project
Giraffe Stories

CHAPTER THREE

TRUST *THEM*? ARE YOU KIDDING? 36

The Importance of Building Trust
How to Build Trust
Efforts to Build Trust Are Risky
Giraffe Stories

CHAPTER FOUR

BUILDING A TEAM AND KEEPING IT TOGETHER 47

How to Build a Team from Scratch
Team Structure
Team Management
Create and Communicate a Team Vision of Success
Giraffe Stories

CHAPTER FIVE

MAKING A PLAN 61

Steps for Visionary Planning
What to Do When Your Plan Succeeds
Giraffe Stories

CHAPTER SIX

RISK TAKING AND COURAGE 76

An Ostrich Nation
Turning It Around—the Giraffe Heroes Project
Turning It Around—Why You Should Take Risks for the Common Good
Tips for Taking Risks as an Active Citizen
Giraffe Stories

CHAPTER SEVEN

FINDING COMMON GROUND:
NEGOTIATING AND RESOLVING CONFLICTS 90

General Principles for Negotiating and Resolving Conflicts
Ten Steps to Common Ground
It Doesn't Work Every Time
Giraffe Stories

CHAPTER EIGHT

PERSUASIVE COMMUNICATIONS:
SPEECHES, FUND-RAISING, AND MORE 118

Persuasive Communications—Style, Attitude, Heart, and Vision
How to Give a Great Speech
Tips for Raising Money
Giraffe Stories

CHAPTER NINE

DEALING WITH THE MEDIA:
THE SECRETS OF GOOD PR 138

Why Should You Tell People What You're Doing?
Creating a Media Strategy
How to Get the Media Results You Want
Giraffe Stories

I WROTE THIS book because I care about the future of our communities and our planet. I wrote it because I have the experience to help solve the public problems that challenge us; I've had failures that have taught me which paths not to take, and successes that have confirmed the ideas and actions that work.

Three key ideas anchor this book:

Courageous and compassionate people can solve any problems and meet any challenges, in their communities and in the world.

The surest path to a meaningful life is service—acting for the common good.

The key to success on this path is balance—head and heart, trust and street smarts, passion and professionalism, reflection and action.

As a young man, I didn't have these ideals or ideas. A Foreign Service Officer for the first 15 years of my professional life, I dealt with conflicts and chaos in the Third World, ignoring the suffering I saw and savoring the adventures. I cultivated a John Wayne image that I really thought was who I was. Then a battle in Vietnam forced me to confront the irresponsibility and shallowness of my life. Gradually I began to change. At the United Nations I finally learned that I could use my skills and experience to build peace and justice rather than their opposites.

I left the Foreign Service in 1980 and began creating a series of workshops helping others to create positive political change in their communities and beyond. In 1983 I merged this work with the Giraffe Heroes Project, an international nonprofit founded the year before by Ann Medlock, a New York writer and editor. Ann was convinced that, in a society grown apathetic and cynical, telling people the stories of real heroes was a powerful way to inspire them to stick their own necks out for the common good. She was right.

The project's strategy was and is simple: We find people already acting with courage and compassion to solve important public problems, and then get the stories of these "Giraffes" told over radio and television and in print. That publicity brings Giraffes attention, support, and—in the case of some Giraffes who are challenging powerful institutions—protection.

But the most important purpose of telling the stories of Giraffes is to move others to follow their lead. People hear or see these compelling stories and are inspired to take action on problems important to *them*. Since 1990 the project also has been using Giraffe stories as the basis for programs for schools, moving young people to lives of courage, compassion, and active citizenship. There's a vast amount of information about this work on the Giraffe Heroes Project Web site (www.giraffe.org).

You'll find stories of Giraffes throughout this book—a sampling of the many hundreds we've honored so far. Giraffes are men, women, and kids, from many races, religions, and backgrounds. They're truck drivers, students, retirees, artists, waitresses, doctors, homemakers, businesspeople, and teachers. Giraffes are working on just about every problem you can think of, from poverty to gang violence to environmental pollution. They're people like

- *Casey Ruud, a safety inspector who put his job on the line when he refused to ignore glaring threats to public safety at the Hanford nuclear plant (see sidebar, page 82);*

- *Ernesto "Neto" Villareal, a high school kid in Idaho who led a campaign to stop racist insults in his school and community (see sidebar, page 8);*

- *Andy and Vashti Hurst, who walked away from a comfortable life to fight poverty, disease, and injustice on the Pine Ridge Indian Reservation (see sidebar, page 10).*

Giraffes are not supermen or superwomen, and they're certainly not saints. They're ordinary people who see a problem and decide to do something about it, despite the risks and obstacles.

At the Giraffe Heroes Project we recognize that inspiration is often not enough, so we provide practical tools that help people translate their inspiration into focused, successful actions. To create these tools, we expanded the three ideas that anchor this book into a set of strategies and techniques that can help anyone make a difference.

I've tested and refined these tools myself, as a diplomat at the United Nations, as an environmental activist helping forge common-ground solutions in land-use battles in the Pacific Northwest, and now as a peacemaker in the Middle East and Africa. I've taught many people how to use these tools in more than 20 years of speeches and workshops for communities, cities, issue groups, companies, government agencies, universities, and labor unions. Now I've put them into this book.

WHO SHOULD READ THIS BOOK

This book is for people who see problems in their communities or beyond and want to help solve them. It's written for people with a wide range of experience and skill:

- *If you're concerned about a public problem but don't have a lot of—or even any—experience to take it on, this book can inspire you to get started, build your skills, guide your steps, and serve as a ready reference.*

- *If you're a seasoned activist, then in this book you'll find challenging new topics, provocative twists on familiar topics, and helpful tips and techniques to add to what you already know. If some of the sections are too basic for you, you'll find them helpful in training others.*

This book is for people acting alone, with small teams, or as members of large organizations. It's for the individual who wants to write a persuasive letter to the editor, for a group of parents concerned about a problem in their kids' school, and for a Sierra Club committee fighting global warming.

This book is for followers—the quiet, behind-the-scenes people who do so much of the work. It's for leaders—the up-front people, including committee chairs, team captains, event organizers, elected officials, and the person who takes responsibility when nobody else does. It's also for people in groups and teams in which leadership is shared.

Finally, while this book focuses on solving public problems, 20 years of giving workshops has taught me that you can use the ideas here in many other areas of your life. No matter what challenges you might take on, the concepts and coaching tips in this book will increase your chances for success. You may be trying to resolve a conflict with a family member, for example, or trying to reach an agreement with a difficult neighbor or cope with a stressful situation at work. This book can help you take the right steps in all those contexts.

HARD AND SOFT

You'll quickly notice a major theme in this book: that creating change as an active citizen requires much more than intellect, energy, and force of will. These hard-edged qualities are needed, but they're not enough. After more than two decades in this work, I'm convinced that treating citizen activism solely as an intellectual and political pursuit is like watching a television set with only one channel—huge amounts of needed insights and information are missing. A large part of this book is about tuning in to those other channels. I've found the following to be true:

- *What most often separates success from failure in active citizenship is a positive and compassionate spirit, as well as competence in the so-called soft skills that flow from such a spirit—such as building trust, communicating with sensitivity, and inspiring others.*

- *Being an active citizen is not just about solving problems. It's also about becoming fully alive—about the meaning and passion you can add to your own life by getting involved. The information in this book not only can change your world, but it can also change your life, as it has done for me and many others.*

HOW TO USE THIS BOOK

The chapters fall into three categories (some into more than one):

■ Action Steps

Chapters 1, 2, 4, and 5 lead you through a progression of moves for creating and carrying out a project, from identifying the problem you want to work on to making a plan to deal with it. These chapters are especially valuable if you are starting from scratch on a new project.

■ Skills Building

Chapters 4, 7, 8, 9, 10, and 11 tell you what you need to know to handle specific challenges, from building a team to dealing with bureaucracies. Some of these chapters are more relevant to your situation than others, depending on the nature of the problem you've taken on.

■ Qualities of Spirit

The first part of chapter 1, chapters 3 and 6, and the epilogue discuss deeper topics relevant to active citizenship, including meaning, trust, courage, connectedness, and responsibility. I've deliberately woven these chapters throughout the book, since that's how I see successful activism working in real life: how-to steps and motivations from the heart melding with and reinforcing each other.

In addition, three ongoing case studies thread through the book, while shorter case studies illustrate specific points.

WHAT'S NOT IN THIS BOOK

There are some standard elements of active citizenship, such as fund-raising, developing Web sites, and incorporating as a nonprofit, on which there are already dozens of existing guides. I saw no point in reiterating that basic information in this book. Instead, I've given you references on these standard topics (see "Resources"), adding my own insights only where I felt they were unique and important.

ACKNOWLEDGMENTS

A group of seasoned activists vetted every chapter of this book, improving what was there and adding their own insights and anecdotes. Between their experience and my own, everything you'll read here has been honed and practiced; nothing is untested theory. This team of persevering people includes Annie Hernandez, Jan Levy, Bill Thorn, Suzanne Sinclair, Dave and Karen Anderson, Steve Scoles, Toby Thaler, Mike Rossotto, Tim Martin, and Diane Kendy.

Thanks also for all the editorial help and encouragement I received from my publishers at Berrett-Koehler. I include especially the two guys at the top, Steve Piersanti and Jeevan Sivasubramaniam, as well as reviewers Steven Slattery, Linda Klatt, Jeffrey Kulick, and Chester Delaney.

I'm especially grateful to Keith Mack and Ann Medlock at Giraffe HQ for their intense and supportive reading of my drafts. They challenged me constantly to make this book better, and I'm embarrassed at how many exaggerations, ambiguities, and lapses of logic they spotted. Also at Giraffe HQ, thanks to Mary Ella Keblusek, Karyn Watkins, Sandy Logan, and Shirley Jantz for their comments and support.

I owe a very special thanks to Evelyn Schaeffer. If ever there was a case of the student teaching the teacher, it's Evelyn and me. She contacted me in 1994 seeking my advice in her challenge of improving phone service in rural Ohio. I offered what advice I could, and for a decade Evelyn improved on it. I'm proud and grateful to include her insights and her anecdotes from her own successful activism.

Thanks also to David Mathews and Noelle McAfee for their contributions on community politics, and to Samuel Halperin for his advice on lobbying.

Writing this book meant assessing hundreds of ideas for creating change, trying to distill them into a message that was concise, consistent, and—above all—helpful. It also meant honestly assessing my own life as an agent for change, acknowledging what had worked and what hadn't. Ann Medlock, the founder of the Giraffe Heroes Project and my wife, supported me in all this from the first page. She moved me to a level of candor, precision, and introspection that I wouldn't have reached on my own. She also let me know every minute that something very good was going to result.

Finally, I acknowledge you, the reader. Whatever your experience level, I trust you'll build on what's in this book and carry it further. My hope is that this guide will serve as an inspiration and a resource for your own lifelong commitment to acting for the common good.

John Graham
Langley, Washington
January 5, 2005

INTRODUCTION

*One of the great liabilities of history is that all too many people
fail to remain awake through great periods of social change.
Every society has its protectors of the status quo and its
fraternities of the indifferent. . . . But today our very survival
depends on our ability to stay awake, to adjust to new ideas, to
remain vigilant and to face the challenge of change.*
MARTIN LUTHER KING JR.

WHAT DO YOU CARE ABOUT?

WHAT ARE THE public problems that
test our times?

At the local level, "public problems"
might include anything that makes your
community less supportive and safe, such
as failing schools, violence, poverty, homelessness, transportation snarls, unwise
development, or corrupt and ineffective
government.

Many of these same problems exist at

USER'S GUIDE

Perhaps for you the problem to
work on is already clear: you
see a pressing challenge that's
not getting handled, for example, or a government or corporate policy you think is dumb or
dangerous. Perhaps you've
already joined an organization
or group working on it. If that's
the case, then you might skip to
chapter 1. If it's *not* clear to you
what problem has your name
on it, however, then read on.

the regional and national levels, in addition to rising health-care
costs, environmental pollution, and shredded social-welfare nets.

And while there are more than enough public problems and challenges at home, we're all citizens of a rapidly shrinking world, where
the effects of globalization, terrorism, and regional conflicts make us
all more aware of just how close—and dangerous—that world is. The
rosy future promised by global free trade has yet to be realized by
most of the world's have-nots, who know very well from television
and the Internet how the other half lives. Warlords in failed states
make violence an everyday event for much of the world's population.
Half the planet is becoming a powder keg of frustrated expectations—
and a recruiting ground for global terrorism.

Behind all these problems is a larger one. The end of the Cold War freed up resources and created unparalleled opportunities to advance the causes of peace and justice, both at home and abroad. Instead, in my view, we've produced a profound and selfish shallowness. Especially in the western world, we've become consumers more than citizens. What happened to the concept of the common good? Of looking beyond the welfare of ourselves and our families and paying serious attention to the welfare of others we may not know, and of the planet we all live on?

KEY POINT ■ *The challenge now is to take responsibility, not just for solving the problems staring us in the face, but for doing so in ways that revive the common good—that bring people closer together instead of pushing them further apart. This book describes those ways.*

WHAT PROBLEM DO *YOU* TAKE ON?

■ Problems in Your Face

Sometimes a problem confronts you in ways that are direct and personal. Giraffe Lois Gibbs, for example, became a crusader against toxic waste when she saw her own kids getting sick (see sidebar, page 4). Here's how some kids found *their* problem, right at their schoolhouse door.

CASE STUDY The Discovery School

The Discovery School, in Coupeville, Washington, is a public school for kids challenged by schoolwork, discipline, or both. Following the Giraffe curriculum then used by the school, the kids asked themselves what problem they cared about most. The choice was easy. Several students had almost been hit by cars that were speeding past the school grounds, ignoring the speed limit to get to the nearby ferry landing. The kids knew that these weren't the only close calls, and that if something wasn't done, somebody was going to get seriously hurt or killed. The lack of traffic safety around their school was the problem they wanted to tackle.

The students started off their project by videotaping speeding cars, clocking them with a stopwatch on a measured distance, and graphing the results. Then they interviewed workers in the area about close calls these people had seen. With that data in hand, they got a state trooper to confirm their findings with his radar gun. They got one of the county commissioners to visit their school to see the problem for himself, and then they made a formal presentation to all the commissioners. The result was a $12,000 traffic light, a crosswalk, and the admiration of everyone who witnessed what they'd accomplished.

■ Suggestions for Your Search

Maybe there isn't a problem right in front of you, but you're open to getting involved if one appears. Don't wait for somebody else to find it for you. Actively seek that challenge important to you and then take it on with everything you've got. Here are some suggestions for your search.

Look around. Look at all the things in your community and country and world that you think aren't going right. For example:

- *Are there people in your community who don't have enough food or who have no shelter?*

- *Are you concerned about the impact of money on politics?*

- *Is the air where you live fit to breathe and the water fit to drink?*

- *Are there global problems that concern you: environmental or economic problems, for example, or human rights problems? In today's interconnected world, local actions, such as consumer boycotts, can have global impacts. It was consumer pressure, for example, that led Home Depot to stop making patio furniture out of wood from old-growth forests overseas.*

Which of these problems do you care most about? Which do you always seem to be talking about with your friends? Which animate your voice and body language?

TRY THIS ■ *Watch the local and national news every night, and read the newspaper. Ask your spouse and friends—and your kids, if you have any—what they think needs fixing. Then make a list of the problems that resonate most with you.*

Take an inventory of your background and experiences, and of what you like to do and what you're good at. Those elements are not in your life as accidents. If you assume, as I do, that there is purpose to existence, then it's hard to avoid the conclusion that personal attributes, whether innate or acquired, are there in order to be used. So if you're really good at working with preschoolers, or giving speeches, or balancing budgets, consider these as indicators of where your path of service may lie.

TRY THIS ■ *Make a résumé—or update the one you have—as if you were applying for a job as an active citizen. Then read it as if you were the "employer." What job would you hire yourself to do?*

Don't rely too much on your mind. The answers you seek will come at least as much from your heart as from your head.

TRY THIS ■ *Take some quiet time and be open to signs, hunches, and intuitive leaps that might help you find your path.*

A GIRAFFE STORY
Lois Gibbs

As a young housewife and mother, Lois Gibbs learned that her Love Canal neighborhood, in Niagara Falls, New York, was built on a toxic-waste dump. Her children were sick, possibly fatally. She had to do something. Gibbs set out to talk to neighbors about what they could do. But she was so unsure of herself that she quit after knocking on one door. Reminding herself that people's lives were at stake, she went back out and knocked on door after door. People called her nuts, or "that hysterical housewife."

"Experts" told her she didn't know what she was talking about, but she kept on, gradually persuading other people to question what was going on and not to trust the corporate polluters and government officials who said that nothing was wrong. Eventually, the effort she started got all 900 families in Love Canal relocated.

Gibbs also went to Congress, where she made sure that what had happened at Love Canal powered a drive to create the Superfund, a multibillion-dollar federal program that forces polluters to clean up their toxic messes.

Gibbs went on to found the Citizens' Clearinghouse for Hazardous Wastes, now called the Center for Health, Environment and Justice, which helps other toxin-plagued communities not only clean up

■ It's Not All or Nothing

Sticking your neck out to help solve public problems—becoming an active citizen—doesn't necessarily mean bailing out of the for-profit world. There are great opportunities in that world, not just to produce needed products at fair prices, but also to provide decent livelihoods for workers, to contribute to communities, and to model what it takes to combine a civic consciousness with a successful bottom line.

It also doesn't necessarily mean upending your life. It may simply mean doing what you do in a different way. Once, after a speech I'd given in Florida, I was stopped in the hall by the publisher of a major newspaper, a man who'd reached the top of his profession in his mid-40s and saw no more peaks to reach. "How can I step down from all this?" he asked. I asked him why he wanted to step down at all. His state was dealing with unchecked growth, racial violence, and a deteriorating environment. What if he were to transform his mission from selling newspapers into helping solve those problems? With a mission of service, he could stay right where he was, stick his neck out, and use his own editorial pages to help create and promote solutions.

Finally, active citizenship is not about being a superhero. It's about starting from where you are, using your talents, personality, enthusiasm, and preferences. You don't have to save the world— maybe the problems that grab your attention are small. Maybe they have to do with some big, pressing social concern, and maybe they don't. Your cause doesn't have to be something intrinsically noble, like feeding the hungry or freeing the oppressed. Most problems are much more "ordinary" than that, but that doesn't mean they are any less worth solving, or that doing so would be any less satisfying.

A GIRAFFE STORY
continued

the poisons, but also work for safe jobs, drinkable water, uncontaminated foods, recycling, and reduction and proper disposal of wastes. The center has an active membership of over 5,000 grassroots organizations and handles about 1,500 requests for assistance every year.

Lois Gibbs went from being a shy housewife, afraid to talk to her neighbors, to being a national leader on an issue of vital concern, all because keeping her family and other families safe from toxic wastes meant so much to her. She didn't find the meaning in her life from getting her picture in the papers—although she did become famous. She found her meaning in service, first to her kids, and then to the nation.

Web link: Center for Health, Environment and Justice (www.chej.org).

I worked with Evelyn Schaeffer, a remarkable activist in rural Ohio whose problem was getting her phone company to provide toll-free calling within Ashtabula County. Schaeffer saw that having to make long-distance calls to people who were nearly neighbors not only ran up the bill, but it also stifled a sense of community. The crusade she led improved the quality of life for a lot of people in one little corner of Ohio. As she wrote recently, "What we did succeeded, and that mattered to me, to all the others who worked on the campaign, and to all those people who still stop me in the street and say, 'You're the lady who got us decent phone service.'"

PLAY IT AGAIN

- *We face many public problems. Behind all of them is the larger challenge of reviving the common good.*

- *Many people never look for a problem to work on—it finds them and won't let go.*

WHAT'S NEXT?
Active citizenship is tough work, and sticking your neck out for what you believe in is, well, risky. Why do it? Why you? Chapter 1 suggests some answers.

- *Look at all the things in your community and country and world that you think aren't going right; maybe one of those problems has your name on it. Local actions, such as consumer boycotts, can have global impacts.*

- *Asking what you care about can help you find a problem to work on. Taking an inventory of your background and experiences, and of what you like to do and what you're good at, will help, too; those elements are no accident. Spend part of your search in silence, and pay attention to signs, hunches, and intuition.*

- *Sticking your neck out to help solve public problems—becoming an active citizen—doesn't require upending your life. It may simply mean doing what you do in a different way. You don't have to save the world; maybe the problems that grab your attention have to do with some big, pressing social concern, and maybe they don't.*

This is the true joy in life, the being used for a purpose
recognized by yourself as a mighty one; the being thoroughly
worn out before you are thrown on the scrap heap; the being
a force of Nature instead of a feverish selfish little clod of
ailments and grievances complaining that the world will
not devote itself to making you happy.
GEORGE BERNARD SHAW,
Man and Superman

WHY DO IT?

WHY HELP YOUR community deal with racism or failing schools? Why press for cleaner air or water, join a neighborhood association, or attend boring hearings on traffic, land use, or homelessness? Why spend hours searching the Web for data on trade or terrorism? Why send letters and e-mails to your congressperson or your mayor? Why stand up to speak your mind when even your friends wish you'd sit down and shut up?

It's hard and often thankless. It takes time you don't have. It's often a hassle.

So why do it? It's a whole lot easier to stay on the sidelines, wanting and expecting "someone" (the government, perhaps?) to solve the problems—meanwhile complaining that things aren't the way you want them to be.

One motivation for getting involved might be sheer frustration and anger over the injustice or incompetence you see. Something isn't working, or someone's being hurt, or some government or company authority keeps making the same mistake over and over again and nobody seems able or willing to get it right. You think, how can they be so stupid/greedy/gutless? Suddenly you've had enough, and you pick up the phone . . .

We all understand that motivation. However, I've been working with activists for over 20 years, and I know that frustration and anger can be great catalysts, but you can't succeed for long if they are your only fuel. *Sooner or later they'll cause you to start making mistakes and missing opportunities.* Eventually they'll undermine your effectiveness, and you'll burn out. There's a stronger, more sustainable motivation for being an active citizen.

When we ask Giraffes—the people honored by the Giraffe Heroes Project—why *they* stick their necks out the way they do, most will say that they were sparked into action by a crisis or problem. But it's also clear that what keeps most Giraffes going over the long haul—and what helps make them as effective as they are—transcends whatever initial frustration and anger they felt. What sustains them is a strong sense that what they're doing to solve that crisis or problem is *meaningful* to them at a profound and personal level; that is, that it's in sync with their deepest priorities and values. When asked about their motivations, many Giraffes just look at us and tell us in so many words that it's a damned-fool question. "The problem was right in front of me," they'll say. "What was I *supposed* to do?" It's almost as if they couldn't *not* do it.

And it isn't just Giraffes who are motivated by a sense of meaning. Philosophers and spiritual leaders have been telling us for millennia that there's no deeper human need and no more powerful yearning than to live a life we know is meaningful. We all want to be able to look at ourselves in the mirror and know that who we are and what we're doing *matters*, that we're not just marking time.

That's certainly true for me. I've lived a while, and my résumé is pretty full. What

A GIRAFFE STORY
Ernesto Villareal

In the small Idaho town of Marsing, football was everything. On Friday nights, hundreds of people from the town and the farms around it would come to watch the Marsing Huskies play. Ernesto "Neto" Villareal was a star player on the high school team, good enough to be considered for a college athletic scholarship.

The problem was the fans. When the players did something good, everyone cheered. But when they made a mistake, something else happened. If the player was Latino, like Villareal, some fans shouted insults like "Stupid Mexican!" It happened a lot, and people seemed not to notice. But the Latino players noticed. Villareal led them in refusing to play anymore unless the insults stopped. Their coach told them that would only make things worse—the team couldn't win the state championship if they stopped playing. Villareal also knew that he could lose his chance at a football scholarship. But stopping the insults meant more than a scholarship. Villareal talked to the student body president, who then talked to the principal. When the principal refused to do anything, the other Latino players were ready to give up and resume playing. Not Villareal. He went over the principal's head to the school board, even though he'd seen one of the school board members shouting insults at Latino players. It

I've found is that I want my actions and commitments to be part of a purpose that satisfies me deep inside and makes me feel totally alive. When I know that what I'm doing is personally meaningful—even if it's very hard—I feel an energy, a sense of excitement, a deep satisfaction of being in the right place at the right time. I'm more inspiring to others, and they are more likely to follow my lead. And I'm much more likely to get the results I want.

WHAT'S YOUR EXPERIENCE? ■ *At home, at work, or in the community, do you feel the difference when you know that what you're doing is meaningful?*

We all know people who involve themselves in activities and relationships that *don't* have meaning for them, or who avoid the search for meaning altogether by pretending that *nothing* is meaningful; they ignore their feelings of emptiness or bury them. It's hard for such people to be creative and to put much focus or energy into what they're doing. They rarely excel; often it's hard for them even to get the job done. People like these are anything but inspiring. It's as if they were slogging through wet concrete.

A GIRAFFE STORY
continued

was difficult, but Villareal told the board why he was refusing to play. "Now," he said to his teammates afterward, "they can't say nobody told them."

The student body president, inspired by Villareal's courage, wrote a letter asking football fans to stop the insults and asking officials to throw people out of the stadium if they didn't stop. Led by Villareal, the Latino players agreed to play only if the letter was read over the loudspeaker at the game.

The principal refused to read the letter, but the school superintendent overruled him and directed that the letter be read. When it was, people in the stadium stood and applauded. And the insults stopped. Neto had scored a touchdown for tolerance. Combating racism in his town meant something to Neto Villareal—and it may have been the biggest win of his career.

Finding what's meaningful to you adds focus, energy, passion, and commitment to your life, and it provides a strong, stable motivation for sticking your neck out as an active citizen.

KEY POINT ■ *The most powerful and positive motivation for getting involved as an active citizen—for creating change that serves the common good—comes from the meaning that the work has for you.*

Finding and doing what makes our lives meaningful also just makes sense. We can expect to be on earth for 80 or so years. Given that finite time, how can we invest our talents, intelligence, and awareness in things we don't find meaningful enough to justify the investment? To me, that's like owning a fancy Swiss watch with no hands. Your life is important, and there's simply got to be more to it than just showing up.

I've been speaking to groups for 20 years, and there's no topic that gets people to lean forward in their seats like this one. The room becomes quiet. No coughs, no shuffling feet. People recognize the feeling and know from their own lives that there is no more important question. Even if buried, unspoken, or denied, the search for meaning drives our lives.

WHAT'S THE PATH TO A MEANINGFUL LIFE?

If meaning is that important, where does it come from and how do you get there?

At the Giraffe Heroes Project, we've written a book for high school kids, and the first thing we talk about is meaning. We know they're living in a culture that would like all of us to believe that our true worth is in what we buy. So we start by asking, "When's the last time something you *bought* made your life meaningful, or even made you feel good for very long?"

That's an important question for all of us, considering that it's adults who create the culture that tries to hook kids on stuff to buy, and we're just as hooked as they are. Maybe for us it's a fancy new car

A GIRAFFE STORY
Andy and Vashti Hurst

Imagine a place about the size of Connecticut, a place that's hot and dusty in the summer and bitterly cold in the winter. It has no resources—no oil, gas, minerals, crops, or lumber. There are no theaters, nursing homes, or public transportation. A third of the houses don't have electricity or running water. Forty thousand people live in this place. Their unemployment rate is upwards of 85 percent. The infant mortality rate is 2.5 times the U.S. average, and the diabetes rate is 8 times higher. The tuberculosis rate is 10 times higher than in nearby areas. Life expectancy matches that of Haiti.

Imagine having to live there. Now imagine choosing to live there. Since 1993 Dr. Andy Hurst and his wife, Vashti, have chosen to live in this desolate place—the Pine Ridge Indian Reservation in South Dakota, in the most prosperous country in the world, in its most prosperous time.

Although the Hursts had enjoyed life in Seattle and New York, they fell in love with the people of Pine Ridge, the Oglala Lakota (Sioux), when they spent a month there as part of Andy's residency program. Now "Doc Andy" provides medical care on the reservation, and the organization the couple founded, the National Association for American Indian Children and Elders (NAAICE), has instead of a knock-'em-dead shirt—but when's the last time something *you* bought put meaning in your life for very long?

Well, if it's not stuff you buy that makes life meaningful, we ask the kids, then what about power and status? At 16, it may be what clique they belong to, but kids can also see older friends and family members who always seem to be headed up some ladder, looking for meaning at the next rung, or the one above that, and not finding it.

Take a look at the people you know who have power or status, we suggest. How many of *them* are leading meaningful lives? And for those who are, is it the power and status that fulfills them—or something else?

So what is a path that gets us there? This story is old, but it makes the point well:

The scene is 13th-century Paris, where construction is in progress on the cathedral of Notre Dame. An onlooker—call him the world's first management consultant—watches three people at work: two stonecutters and an old woman who sweeps up the broken pieces of stone.

The consultant asks the first stonecutter what he's doing. The man says, "I'm cutting stones, and that puts meat and potatoes on the table for my family."

The consultant asks the same question of the second stonecutter, who answers, "I'm making a gargoyle for the top of the west buttress."

Then the consultant asks the old woman what she's doing. She stops moving her broom and turns to look at the place in the sky where the great spires will eventually rise, decades after she is dead.

created 30 support programs. These include programs for home ownership and for renovating homes and service facilities; for building wheelchair ramps, playgrounds, vegetable gardens, and outhouses; for distributing food, clothing, fuel, furniture, school supplies, Christmas gifts, and new-baby supplies; for running a basketball camp; and for managing volunteers who come from far and wide to work on NAAICE projects.

Perhaps even more important, the Hursts have become messengers to the rest of America, sounding the alarm about the dire situation at Pine Ridge and drumming up concern and concrete aid.

"We need to reverse our history of genocide against First Nations people, to see our own human rights issues instead of just pointing the finger at other countries," says Andy Hurst. "We must help these good people."

The Hursts will tell you they've gained more than they've expended in aiding the people of Pine Ridge—they gain every time an Oglala Lakota begins living a better life.

When Vashti Hurst is asked why they persist, she says, "Why do we go on? Because *they* go on. They are people of great dignity and grace. We know that other Americans will help when they realize what a crisis this is."

Then she turns back and says, "I, sir, am helping build a great cathedral where people can be with God."

That old woman had it right. She had found meaning for her life—not in possessions or positions, but in seeing her menial job as a commitment to a task bigger than herself and her own needs.

We get the same lesson from Giraffes. People like Ernesto Villareal, who took on school officials to combat racism in his community (see sidebar, page 8), or Andy and Vashti Hurst, who dedicated their lives to providing medical help and fighting for justice in the poorest place in America (see sidebar, page 10).

KEY POINT ■ *People who lead meaningful lives—like that old woman, like Giraffes—don't find that meaning in possessions or positions;* they find it in carrying out personal commitments to ideals bigger than themselves and their own needs. *It's this* commitment *that generates the personal enthusiasm, passion, and power of a meaningful life.*

That's true for Giraffes. I think it's true for anyone.

But there are many ideals that transcend individual needs. Some of them are negative: The Nazis found meaning in their commitment to ruling Europe. Suicide bombers give their lives for a cause. There may be enthusiasm, passion, and power in commitments like these, but their success depends on the defeat of others, who are certain to fight back. Eventually it's a downward spiral.

KEY POINT ■ *There is a way to find meaning that is positive and lasting. And that's to commit to ideals of service, of working for the common good. The old woman was building a place where people could be with God. Giraffes are, one and all, acting for the good of their communities and beyond.*

It took me a long time to get this lesson.

When I was a teenager and young man, the only thing that held meaning for me was adventuring. I shipped out on freighters while still in high school. I was part of a team that made the first ascent of the north wall of Mt. McKinley in Alaska, a climb so dangerous it's never been repeated. I hitchhiked around the world. As a correspondent for The Boston Globe in the mid-'60s, I waded into every shooting war I could find, from Algeria to Laos. The only thing that mattered was the next adrenaline rush.

Then I joined the U.S. Foreign Service. I was a diplomat for 15 years and moved up the ladder fast. I worked not in embassies but in jungles and deserts all over the Third World. I was in the revolution in Libya in 1969, then in Vietnam for a year and a half. I'd asked for Vietnam, not because I thought the war was right or just, but because being in a war was an adventure I'd not yet had. And doing a good job in a dangerous place meant rapid promotions.

Home from the war, I became one of the fastest-rising stars in the Foreign Service. Most of my work dealt with wars and revolutions and arms sales. I saw oppression, hunger, and war all over the world; what held meaning for me, however, was not an urge to relieve the suffering, but the attraction of danger in those far-off spots and my own surging career. The most important day of the year for me was the day when the promotion list came out. When my name was on it, I went out to celebrate.

By the time I was 35, however, the motivations for what I was doing with my life began to sit in the pit of my stomach like a bad meal. *Nothing* seemed meaningful to me anymore—not in any sense that felt right or fulfilling.

CASE STUDY **At the United Nations**

In the late 1970s, my career took me to the U.S. Mission to the United Nations. Part of my job there was overseeing the arms embargo on South Africa. It had been imposed because much of the military equipment sold to the South African government in those years was used to enforce apartheid.

But the embargo leaked like a sieve; there were huge amounts of money involved in the arms trade, and the arms dealers had their friends in parliaments in Europe and in our own Congress. I ignored my instructions to overlook the leaks in the embargo and instead worked secretly for months to tighten it. I did that by helping Third World countries increase their pressure against my own government.

It worked. A tougher embargo was enforced, which helped end apartheid. At any time in this process I could have been fired for insubordination or worse—and almost was.

I took those risks because of a day in South Africa that started with meetings with black activists in the squalor and oppression of the black township of Soweto, and ended with a diplomatic cocktail party in Johannesburg's fanciest white suburb, in a mansion surrounded by wrought-iron fences and guard dogs.

Apartheid stank. From that afternoon on, helping end apartheid *meant* something to me at some far deeper place in my soul than self-centered adventures and promotions. Like Giraffes, *I couldn't not do what I did.*

The arms embargo only whetted my appetite. I quickly discovered that I could take all the skills I'd been using to play political power games and focus them instead on peace and justice issues in the Third World.

This discovery made all the difference—to the people I was helping, and to me. At the UN I'd finally found what it was that could make my life meaningful. It wasn't chasing adventure or status or power; it was working to end injustice and suffering. Being part of the efforts to end apartheid, to bring freedom to colonies in Africa and Asia, and to press for human rights pulled me to a new focus for my life. Ironically, the thrill of making a difference this way matched the thrill of any adventures I'd ever had, and it was satisfying in a way no promotion had ever been.

This story may be exotic, but the point is not. I think the path to a meaningful life is out there for each of us, but we have to find it. I tell people, especially young people, what I wish I'd been told when I was just starting out: that every one of us has and will have unique opportunities to make a difference, if only in small and quiet ways. A successful life is about spotting those opportunities and acting on them. The only mistake you can make is to ignore the quest, to settle for an ordinary life, to just look out for Number One, to grow up and live and die without ever having made a difference.

TRY THIS ■ *Take the time and the risk to ask yourself some tough questions and to reflect on the answers:*

■ *Is what I'm doing with my life, including any current volunteer work, meaningful enough to me, or am I just going through the motions?*

■ *What ideals am I committed to—or might I commit to—to provide that meaning?*

■ *What more can I do to put those ideals into action?*

Ask yourself these questions regularly. If you're satisfied that an activity has meaning for you, keep reminding yourself that it does. Never take it for granted. Never refer to your work as a citizen activist as a "duty." Call it what it is—something that makes you fully alive.

And if introspection tells you that you are stuck in something without enough meaning for you, then commit yourself to changing that.

GOING FOR IT

Citizenship is not a spectator sport. It means more than just wishing something good might happen or cheering someone else on. It's more than turning out to vote once in a while. It means investing your time, energy, and resources to make a difference. If we fail to do this—if we consistently wait for others to solve the problems we see—then we muffle our voices, abdicate our responsibilities, and have little right to complain if things turn out badly.

There is an issue out there with your name on it, something you care about, someplace where you can serve and make a difference. Whatever it is, large or small, pay attention to it.

And if you've been energized by a single project, don't stop there. Use what you learned the first time around to help others tackle the same problem—or to take on other causes that might benefit from your experience and contacts. When the poisoning of Love Canal put her own kids in danger, Giraffe Lois Gibbs acted to stop that threat (see sidebar, page 4). But after she won at Love Canal, she started a national organization to help all communities threatened by toxic wastes.

Not long ago I went back for a reunion of the prep school in Tacoma, Washington, from which I had graduated. Nearly all my classmates were leading comfortable lives in business or the professions. They talked about portfolios and college tuitions. I was bored to death—except by one man. His name was Tom Noble. A poor student and slow of speech in high school, he'd been the butt of jokes. But for the past 30 years he'd been directing a social-services agency in the worst area of Tacoma and had just started a controversial needle-exchange program.

Tom Noble was fascinating. He spoke with the charisma and energy and peace of mind of a person who had truly found his calling and answered it with everything he had.

The poet Mary Oliver asks, "Tell me, what is it you plan to do with your one wild and precious life?"

It's the most important question you'll ever ask yourself.

Use your one wild and precious life to serve a cause you believe in. Get involved. The rest of this book will help you do that with courage and skill.

PLAY IT AGAIN

WHAT'S NEXT?
When you've found the issue with your name on it, the next steps are to learn all you can about it, design a specific project, and create a vision for its success.

- *The most powerful and positive motivation for sticking your neck out as an active citizen comes from the meaning that this work has for you.*

- *People who lead meaningful lives don't find that meaning in possessions or positions; they find it in carrying out personal commitments to ideals bigger than themselves and their own needs—especially ideals of service, of working for the common good.*

- *There is an issue out there with your name on it, something you care about, someplace where you can serve and make a difference.*

- *If you've been energized by a single project, don't stop there. Use what you've learned the first time around to help others tackle the same problem—or to take on other causes that might benefit from your experience and contacts.*

- *Active citizenship means more than just wishing something good might happen or cheering someone else on. It means investing your own time, energy, and resources. Ignore this and you muffle your voice, abdicate your responsibilities, and weaken your right to complain if things turn out badly.*

CHAPTER TWO

It's kind of fun to do the impossible.
WALT DISNEY

START HERE

ASSUMING YOU'VE identified the problem you'd like to take on, start with these first two steps:

■ *Research the problem.*

■ *Decide the form of your participation—you can join an existing organization or launch your own effort, either by yourself or by forming a group.*

RESEARCH

At this stage, you don't need to become an expert. But you do need to learn enough about your problem to know what you might be getting into.

■ Find Out if There Are Groups Already Organized to Work on This Problem

They could be advocacy organizations, government agencies, professional associations, service clubs, or political groups. Use your favorite Web search engine. Ask friends. Check newspapers and magazines. Maybe a piece of your junk mail is from a like-minded group. If and when you find such a group, download or send for its information. If it's local, attend a meeting and ask questions.

▪ Be Skeptical

There may be no organized groups with information you can readily tap. And even if there are, they're very likely to describe the problem from just their point of view. So do some independent research. Along the way, *be skeptical* (especially of people who tell you that nothing can be done), and be relentless in pursuing the information you need.

CASE STUDY Ashtabula County, Ohio

In 1993, when Evelyn Schaeffer took on the local phone company to get it to provide toll-free calling within her rural Ohio county, she knew next to nothing about the challenge she'd taken up. Eleven years later she writes:

> I think it's generally true that the research initially shows that it can't be fixed—if it was easy, the problem wouldn't still be there. Initial questions about the problem are addressed to people who "know" about it, and that's where you really have to have enough passion in you not to accept what you are told, even from people you really respect. I started out asking about the phone situation and was told by execs in the local company all about technical things I didn't understand.

> I spent a lot of hours just being stubborn, with a kind of "there has to be a way" mentality, until I'd assembled enough information and learned enough technical stuff that I could see the inconsistencies in what people were telling me as "truths."

▪ Use Multiple Sources

Go to the Web. Go to the library. Join organizations working on this problem. If your problem is local, find and talk to people both inside and outside organized groups who may have expertise and experience in dealing with it—academics, authors, and reporters, for example. Are there other communities, cities, and so on, with identical or similar problems? Talk to them. You'll learn something—and it may even make sense to join forces with them.

■ Research the History of the Problem

When did it become a problem, and why? Were there past efforts to tackle it? If so, what happened? Even if the work went nowhere, it may have made some progress or unearthed some information you can use. And finding out why it died may show you some important pitfalls to avoid.

■ Identify the "Stakeholders"

These will include

- *people whose lives are directly affected;*

- *people indirectly affected (such as taxpayers, for any issue involving public funds);*

- *people charged with making the decisions regarding this problem;*

- *people who can influence the decision makers (such as technical experts and consultants, and the media).*

■ Learn the Vocabulary of This Problem and How It Affects the Discussion

Significant problems tend to develop a language of their own. People involved in the abortion issue, for example, tend to define their positions as either "pro-life" or "pro-choice." Talk to people who've been involved in the problem that concerns you, to learn the subtleties and any pitfalls in the words used to describe it.

■ Listen to Groups or Individuals *Opposed* to What You Want to See Happen

Assess their information and learn from it—there's always at least one other side. How does your state justify clear-cutting in state forests? Why did your city council shoot down funds for public transportation? Read the speeches of the person you are *not* going to vote for.

▪ Gain at Least a Beginner's Handle on Any Technical Background Important to This Problem

Just how toxic is that roadside spray you oppose, and what are the credentials of your sources? How does your state make decisions on transportation, and who makes them and when? What's the effect on small businesses and farms of eliminating the federal estate tax?

▪ Examine the "Iceberg"

Problems are like icebergs—the part that's under the water is a lot bigger than the part you can see. The visible part is what people talk about easily. But the real problems are almost always deeper, below the waterline, and not so easy to talk about, especially if some of those deeper issues are your own.

Part of what's down there is hidden agendas. For example, a city council might blame budget woes for not extending mass transit from the inner city to the more affluent suburbs. But a real, if unstated, reason might be a fear that extending mass transit would bring with it inner-city criminals and crime.

Not everything below the waterline of a problem is as conscious and deliberate as a hidden agenda. With a contentious problem, you might be dealing with people who are carrying personal baggage—such as anger or resentment or fear of change—created by events and histories that may have no direct connection to what's on the table.

WHAT'S YOUR EXPERIENCE? ▪ *Think of some complex problem you've been involved with that just wouldn't go away. Were there people involved—maybe you were one of them—with some history that was never on the table but that made dealing with what was on the table much more difficult?*

We'll talk about how to deal with iceberg situations later, especially in the discussions in chapter 7 on negotiating and resolving conflicts. For now, think about the iceberg image and consider that, in doing your research, what you see on the surface is almost never the whole story. You'll want to get below the waterline of your issue as best you can.

■ At This Early Stage, Don't Be Afraid to Bail Out

In the course of this initial research, when your investment is small, you may find that this problem was not so much your problem to solve as you had thought. If that happens, drop back and find another one. It's out there. But if and when you're satisfied that this *is* your problem, and you've done some initial research, including independent digging, then . . .

DECIDE THE *FORM* OF YOUR PARTICIPATION

In the course of your research, you may have found a like-minded organization doing pretty much what you want to do. If what it's doing offers opportunities for you to make a satisfying contribution, there may be no need to start a project of your own. If it's local or if there's a local chapter of a larger group, then attend a meeting. If not, contact the group's headquarters and begin exploring how you can get involved.

But what if you don't find a group already working on your problem? Or what if you find a group, but its interest in your problem is peripheral, or you're not comfortable with other parts of its agenda, or you don't like the people running it, or for any other reason you don't see a good match? If you're determined to keep going, your choice now is to either make do with the imperfect fit or launch your own effort.

If you decide to go your own way and the problem is not so large, you might choose to start by working alone. That will remove some potential headaches—you get to call all the shots. But even the simplest of problems has a way of expanding beyond one person's time, resources, and abilities to deal with it, so be prepared to expand the project into a team effort if and when you need to do that (see chapter 4). By yourself or with a team you form, here are the next steps you'll need to take:

■ *Create a specific project.*

■ *Create a vision for its success.*

■ *Add enough details so that you can begin to plan.*

CREATE A SPECIFIC PROJECT

Choosing the problem answers the question "What do I care about?" "Violence in my kid's school" and "Ugly sprawl taking over my town" are examples of problems.

But problems are often broad and diffuse—great for inspiring action but not so great for providing detailed guidance. So after you've done basic research on the *problem*, the next step is to create a specific *project* that helps solve it—something you can plan and implement with the time and resources you've got or can get. Creating the project answers the question "How, specifically, can I make a difference?" A good project has a vision, goals, timelines, and a budget. "Creating a conflict-resolution program in my kid's school" and "Getting the town council to pass an anti-sprawl ordinance" are examples of projects created in response to the problems cited above.

KEY POINT ■ *Choose the problem before creating the project—but don't ignore either step.*

Swinging into action with only the problem burning in your heart, and without a defined project, is too unfocused to produce a good result. On the other hand, launching a project not linked to some underlying problem you care about risks undermining the clarity and enthusiasm you need to succeed.

Here are steps for creating your project:

Sarah Swagart

Back when she was an eighth-grader, Sarah Swagart decided it was wrong for young skateboarders to be treated like criminals in her town, Oak Harbor, Washington. Kids who "skated" in Oak Harbor's parking lots and on its sidewalks were threatened with fines of as much as $500 and 90 days in jail. Swagart, not a skateboarder herself, could see that the kids might be annoying but they definitely didn't deserve treatment like that. The skaters were nobody special, she thought—just boys who needed a place to exercise their sometimes awesome skills.

Swagart formed Nobody Special, an organization whose mission was to get the skateboarders their own place to practice—and to get the community to recognize them as athletes, not hoodlums.

She shared her vision with a local architect, who volunteered to design a skateboard park. But there had to be someplace to put it. Swagart realized that no matter how much it scared her to speak in public, she had to start talking if the kids were going to get some land and build their park. She drew up a petition for land and got signatures from kids, teachers, police officers, and even some store owners. Leading a delegation of 40 kids, she stood before the city council and pointed out that the town

■ Review the Research You've Done about the Problem

Who's already involved? What's the history and who are the stakeholders? What does the "other side" have to say? What's below the waterline?

■ Discuss Ideas for Projects with Friends and Potential Allies

What could you (or a group you start) do that would make a difference? Involving others at this early stage is more than a means of generating ideas—you may well attract people who'll stick around to work with you.

■ Think about the *Scope* of Any Project You Might Create

Projects, and commitments to projects, have a way of expanding once the action starts. How much time, energy, and resources are you personally willing to put in now? How might the work expand, and how far would you be willing to go with it if it does? You'll want to steer away from projects that are clearly out of reach—but don't settle for something that's too cautious either. Don't veto projects that require money, volunteers, or other resources you don't now have. You can get all those things as part of the work.

■ Take Stock of Your Own Talents, Skills, Experience, Likes, and Dislikes

Whatever project you decide on should make good use of who you are. Trying to put a square peg in a round hole is not a great way to start. If you can't draw, then launching an arts project for inner-city kids might not be the best choice for you. On the other hand, if you're a marine biologist, then leading beach walks for those kids might be perfect.

A GIRAFFE STORY

continued

had baseball fields, basketball courts, a roller rink, and a swimming pool where kids could do the sports of their choice. What would be so different about accommodating the skateboarders?

The city council agreed that there could be a park next to the public swimming pool. Then Swagart and the skateboarders got a commitment from the Seabees at nearby Whidbey Naval Air Station to do the construction work. They got local businesses to donate materials. And they organized a series of events to raise the rest of the money needed. The skaters' park is now a reality.

- ## Weigh the Conflicts You Are Almost Certain to Generate

If you take on a project that's not going to be universally popular, you will be criticized. How big is your comfort zone on conflict, and are you ready to expand it if you have to? See chapter 7.

- ## Don't Expect to Have All the Details in the Beginning

You'll refine your project as you go forward with it. What you want at this stage is a decent outline of your project—something from which you can launch the vision that will supply the inspiration and clarity you need for its success.

CASE STUDY The Island County Citizens'
Growth Management Coalition

The Problem

Since the early 1970s, the quality of life that's made Washington State such a desirable place to live has been disappearing. Unprecedented population growth and sprawl have taken away thousands of acres of forests and farmland. Critical wetlands and wildlife habitat have been lost to development. Existing conservation rules for shorelines have been inadequate to protect salmon and the smaller fish they feed upon. All of these concerns directly threaten Island County, a small rural county consisting of two islands an hour north of Seattle. It's where my wife, Ann, and I have lived since 1985. The county's future is something we both care very much about.

The Research

It quickly became clear that the problem of preserving the rural character and environmental health of Island County was complex. While there were local environmental groups working on isolated parts of the problem by the mid-'90s, there was no existing group—and certainly no individual—with the skills and scope to take on the whole problem.

Part of the initial research involved gaining at least a layman's handle on the science dealing with streams, wetlands, aquifers, and habitat. Fortunately, there was plenty of information available from national and statewide environmental groups, from academic books and papers, from experts at nearby universities, and—as time went by—on the Web.

The legal problems were equally complex. Alarmed by the impact of growth, the Washington State Legislature in 1990—91 had passed the Growth Management Act (GMA), which called on the fastest-growing cities and counties, including Island County, to adopt "Comprehensive Plans" for their growth over a 20-year time span. Each city and county was given considerable flexibility to create a "Comp Plan" that fit local conditions, as long as it met key anti-sprawl goals set by the state. Because the legislature had avoided precise prescriptions, court interpretations and precedents that defined the GMA also became very important and had to be studied.

There were also intense political and social factors in Island County on which much depended. For decades a good-old-boy network had done pretty much what it wanted with land development in the county, and GMA or not, it was determined not to give up its freedom to act. While some professional developers shared concerns about sprawl and overdevelopment, many continued to work hand in glove with the good old boys to keep the county's rules for land development as few and as weak as possible.

Demographics were running against the old-timers, however, and many people had moved to the islands (my wife and me among them) with quite different views on the need for combating sprawl and preserving environmental values. So understanding local political and social realities, and how to influence local public opinion and elections, was key in any effort to take on this problem. Much of this homework involved talking to local opinion makers and to ordinary citizens from all quarters who had watched the county grow and change.

Finally, there were problems below the waterline that constantly threatened to sabotage progress. These included fear of change, greed, class problems, deep-seated angers and animosities from past battles, and visceral allegiance by some to ideologies of both the left and the right. In short, beautiful Island County was a minefield, and if you didn't know about, and take into account, the hidden agendas and buried emotions and prejudices, there was no way to navigate it successfully.

The Form of Participation

When Ann and I saw the threats posed by overdevelopment to the place we called home, we understood immediately that no one person could stop it. Within a year or so after our arrival, we helped organize a group called Citizens for Sensible Development (CSD), which quashed the heedless expansion of a local airport and also focused local attention on Island County's fragile water supplies. When the Growth Management Act was passed, however, it meant that *every* aspect of county land use had to be reviewed and decided anew, and CSD was too small to watchdog a task that big. The same was true for the other half-dozen environmental organizations in the county, each with its own unique focus, resources, and membership. We were all faced with Ben Franklin's famous dictum: we would hang together or we would hang separately. In mid-1997 we pooled our resources to form the Citizens' Growth Management Coalition.

The Project

Island County's commissioners, kept in power by the entrenched interests, had for years balked at creating a Comprehensive Plan to meet the growth management criteria mandated by the state legislature. In 1997, threatened with economic sanctions by the governor, the commissioners finally hired consultants and got serious about completing a plan that, even if it failed to meet some growth management goals, might at least reduce the immediate threat of economic sanctions.

Doubting that the county on its own would make the tough decisions needed to comply with the Growth Management Act, the coalition created a project whose goal was "to ensure that the County's emerging Comp Plan complied with the GMA, protected the environment, retained the rural character of the County and planned for enough jobs, housing, water and other infrastructure to sustain current and future residents."

CREATE A VISION FOR YOUR PROJECT'S SUCCESS

A vision is a mental picture of the result you want to achieve—a picture so clear and strong it will help make that result real. A vision is not a vague wish or dream or hope. It's a picture of the real results of real efforts. It comes from the future and informs and energizes the present.

The practice of using visions is mainstream. Some companies use visions to communicate their values and goals. Professional sports teams use visioning exercises to improve performance (there are studies showing that basketball players who practice free throws only by "envisioning" the ball going through the hoop improve their shooting percentage almost as much as those who actually throw the ball). The director of a play might "envision" a perfect production before rehearsals begin.

This section describes the why and how of creating a vision. This information is useful whether you're creating a project on your own or you're joining a group already organized around a project. Later in the book, I'll show you how to communicate your vision to a group or team, pulling in volunteers and resources. I'll also explain how to use a vision to guide your planning process, to get institutions and bureaucracies to listen to you, and to shape your communications—from speeches to brochures.

■ Why Visions Are Important

KEY POINT ■ *Visioning is the most powerful tool I've witnessed in more than 20 years of helping organizations and individuals get the results they want.*

One of the most famous visions in U.S. history was that of Martin Luther King Jr. When he said, "I have a dream," there was very little national support for his cause, and Congress showed no signs of passing civil rights legislation. But Dr. King's vision catalyzed progress—in attitudes, strategy, actions, and legislation—where there had been none.

A vision inspires action. As in Dr. King's case, a powerful vision pulls in ideas, people, and other resources. It creates the energy and will to make change happen. It inspires individuals and organizations to commit, to persist, and to give their best. Giraffe Sarah Swagart used her vision to attract the help she needed to make that vision a reality (see sidebar, page 22).

A vision is a practical guide. Use it for creating plans, setting goals and objectives, making decisions, and coordinating and evaluating the work on any project, large or small. A vision is like true north on the compass—no matter what decisions on a project need to be made, you can test each option by asking if it will help attain the vision set for that project.

A vision helps keep organizations and groups focused and together. This is especially true with complex projects and in stressful times. A vision is a kind of glue, helping people in groups stay committed to a common goal, especially when there might be temptations and pressures to bail. If people share a vision, it's easier for them to see connections between what they want as individuals and the goals of the entire group.

Have you ever been in a group that spends an hour arguing over a small problem, like what color paper to use for a brochure? That's a group that needs a vision. When there's a clear, sharp, shared vision, a group doesn't get bogged down in trivia; the small stuff just gets handled because everybody can see and appreciate the bigger picture of where the group is going.

▪ Not Every Picture Is a Vision

A vision should do the following things:

Be clear. It should be so sharp and so detailed that you can see, smell, and taste the smallest details. If your vision is teaching a kid to read, picture her getting

When an environmental group was working to stop a big coal-fired power plant from being built near the Grand Canyon, Michael Stewartt, a private pilot, had an idea: he and some pilot friends flew reporters and photographers over the proposed plant site so that they could see for themselves how close it was to the canyon. It worked. The controversy created by the media stories forced the power company to scrap its plans.

The Grand Canyon flyover worked so well that Stewartt envisioned volunteer pilots providing the same service for other areas endangered by pollution or clear-cutting. He got a wealthy Colorado rancher to share his vision of an environmental "eye in the sky." The rancher let Stewartt use one of his planes and enough gas for 150 hours of flying. The new organization, LightHawk, was off the ground.

In the early years, Stewartt and another pilot worked primarily with conservationists in the Rocky Mountains and with Arizona's Smelter Crisis Education Project (SCEP), laying the groundwork for a success that would really put wind beneath LightHawk's wings.

For 40 years, a copper smelter in Arizona had had the dubious distinction of contributing to more acid rain and air pollution than any other plant in the United States. When Light-Hawk photographed the through a whole page by herself for the first time, right down to the little catches in her voice and the huge grin that lights up the room when she's done. If your vision is achieving a personal best in running a race, feel the air rushing past your ears and hear the shouts urging you on. Hear the applause when you cross the finish line and look up at the clock to see that you've done your best time ever.

Be positive. Acknowledge the difficulties, but don't try to motivate yourself or others with a vision of bad things that might happen if you don't succeed. A vision that builds people's fears may help fuel immediate action, but it can also cripple creative and courageous thinking.

Be big enough. Create a bigger picture of the effects of your work than just solving the problem at hand. For example, see your hard work and commitment inspiring others to follow your lead in addressing the same problem in other places. See the lessons you learn informing others working on similar projects elsewhere. See your results added to other results to achieve widespread change. Don't lose your focus and commitment on the challenge where you are—but do allow yourself to develop a vision of the full scope of what you can achieve.

A vision that's too small may not provide enough inspiration or generate enough energy to get you past the tough spots. It might even close your mind to what you *could* achieve. In the Citizens' Growth Management Coalition in Island County, for example, we saw from the

emissions from the smelter, helping SCEP get it shut down, conservationists realized they had a powerful new ally. Stewartt's vision of what concerned pilots like himself could do to save wilderness areas was becoming a reality. The organization grew to 30 active volunteer pilots who have their own planes and can give fast support to environmentalists.

The impact has been enormous. After a powerful politician who was a longtime timber-industry advocate flew over Vancouver Island with Stewartt, she began calling for an immediate end to clearcutting. In Alaska, LightHawk spent a week flying legislators, conservationists, and reporters over the Tongass National Forest, America's largest rain forest. In the waters off the many islands and peninsulas they saw orcas, otters, dolphins, and humpback whales. On land, there were grizzly bears and wolves. But in the clear-cut patches where ancient old-growth Sitka spruce once stood, they saw silt-choked streams where fish could no longer live. That enlightening week helped start the ball rolling on a repeal of the U.S. Forest Service rules that allowed wholesale clear-cutting in the Tongass.

Stewartt's vision grew to include flying in Southeast Asia and Costa Rica and producing television ads on the crisis in the rain forests.

Web link: LightHawk (www.lighthawk.org/vp.htm).

start that sharing our extensive research on land-use problems over the Internet could help create a statewide pattern of change. Giraffe Michael Stewartt's vision grew from combating one local environmental abuse to a worldwide campaign (see sidebar, page 28).

Include changes in attitudes. Remember the iceberg! The challenge you see in front of you is only the part of the problem you can see—the rest of the challenge is deeper and often involves personal attitudes that may be strongly held. That's why effective, long-lasting solutions demand changes in people's attitudes. Any strategy that ignores attitudes is likely to be a short-term fix—the "solved" problem will reappear, often in a different form.

Include a clear picture of your personal role. This isn't about ego. It's about your taking full responsibility for helping achieve the results you want. It's you out of the stands and onto the playing field.

Come from the heart, not the head. Don't try to think your way to a vision. To create a vision that's exciting and compelling, you've got to give yourself the freedom to dream—to use your imagination to see and feel what does not yet exist. Put yourself into the future and look back. It's easier to do that during a long, quiet walk than over a yellow pad.

A vision is not the same as goals or objectives; they come from the head and are very important at a later stage in the planning process (see chapter 5); they flow *from* a vision and guide the specific steps that will make it real.

▪ What's the Vision for Your Project?

The following instructions are for creating a vision with a group, but you can easily adjust them if you are visioning on your own.

Start by reviewing everything you know about your problem and about the project you intend to take on. Then pick a date in the future when your project will have just finished.

Ask everyone to put themselves into the future at that date and at the place where the results of the project are most evident. They can close their eyes if that makes this process easier. The project has been a huge success. Ask everyone to spend a few minutes "seeing" that success. Start with any new or different buildings, equipment, or events. Ask everyone to describe in their minds the people they see, right down to the color of their socks. What new sounds and smells are there—kids laughing, hot dogs cooking . . . ? If there's media coverage, describe it. Let the images flood in. How do the people affected by this project feel about it? How have their attitudes changed? What are they saying? What does their body language tell you? How do *you* feel about this success? Ask group members to keep drawing more and more detailed mental pictures, always keeping themselves in the future, looking out and looking back.

Now split people up into pairs, and ask each person to spend three minutes describing his or her vision to a partner. *They are in the future*, so the only hard and fast rule of this exercise is never to use the future tense. It's not "We *will prevent* a cut in state education funding" but "We *have prevented* a cut in state education funding."

When everyone has described a vision, ask them all (still in the future) to look backward and silently reflect: before their project started, what were the three biggest obstacles they faced? At least one of these obstacles must have been an unhelpful attitude on the part of someone involved (maybe the person visioning!).

When everybody's got three obstacles, ask them, again in pairs (looking back and not forward), to describe what those three obstacles were and how they overcame them. Urge people not to slow down by trying to analyze or ponder—just let the pictures flow. The project *did* succeed, so obviously the obstacles were overcome. How did that happen? Just start talking. People will be surprised at how many good problem-solving ideas appear. (When you move on to actually planning and carrying out your project in chapter 5, what you've gained from this technique will help you see obstacles not as insurmountable, but as similar to the hurdles you've already jumped in your vision.)

Finally, pull people back to the present and ask for volunteers to describe their visions, including the obstacles they had to overcome to get there. Write (or draw) these pictures on a flip chart or blackboard. Discuss them, noticing which ones come up most often. Then start pooling all these vision elements into a composite picture that fairly represents the vision of the whole group. Put that picture into a *vision statement*. A short, relatively cohesive paragraph is usually enough, but there's no word limit. If you wish, illustrate what you've written with drawings or photographs. Again, you are *not* writing goals and objectives—that comes later, when we get to the from-the-head stuff.

I've done this visioning exercise with hundreds of audiences, and I can't count the number of real and successful projects that have benefited from it. But if you're still skeptical, practice on smaller, private projects first—little things you want to happen in your own life at home or at the office, for example. Go through the process above. You'll gain confidence that it works. I guarantee you that a strong vision will consistently raise the odds of your success on any kind of project.

CASE STUDY Island County

After we chose our problem, did initial research, and created our project, the next step for the Growth Management Coalition was to create a vision for the results we wanted. We chose 20 years as the end point for our vision, since that was the planning horizon set by the state. So we put ourselves 20 years into the future and "walked" or "drove" in our minds from one end of the county to the other. We saw, for example, how our towns had grown in people-friendly ways, how farms were prospering, and how habitat and environmental values had been conserved.

We then condensed all these pictures into a short vision statement and published it, both as a guide and inspiration for ourselves, and as a way of presenting an attractive, balanced picture of the future that would encourage our allies and convert at least some of our opponents. Through the next three years, that vision lent power and focus to everything we did. Especially when we hit rough spots, the coalition's vision helped keep us moving forward.

Here's the coalition's vision statement:

"It is 2020. Island County is a rural oasis, and a model for other places fighting to curb overdevelopment and sprawl in the crowded Puget Sound area. Even in our towns, we live with the sounds of frogs, owls, and coyotes and with the sight of mountains, prairies, water, and stars. We breathe clean air. We smell evergreens, saltwater, and manure. We drink clean water. For most of us, our travel is over country roads, past forests and pastures and working farms. Our economy is soundly grounded in our ruralness, including tourism, retirees' investments in real estate and services, and the payrolls of small-scale businesses attracted here by our rural style. Some of us are farmers and foresters, making our livings off our lands, and supplying County residents with fresh vegetables and meats. Our communities are pedestrian-oriented and people-friendly. There is good housing for all of us, good schools for our kids, and thriving arts communities. There are vigorous debates on many problems, but we do a good job of respecting divergent views and of focusing on what unites us rather than the opposite. We all see our home here as rural, and we are willing to act and vote in ways that keep it that way."

ADD DETAILS TO YOUR PROJECT

Creating a vision should have sparked some new thinking about your project. What, exactly, does this project have to accomplish in order to make its vision real? What you need now is enough details so that you can begin to form an action plan (chapter 5). The list won't be complete, and that's OK—you'll add to it and refine it as you go.

You may also want to come up with an energizing name for your project—something that tells what the project is, conveys energy and commitment, and appeals to all the people who will hear about it or be involved in it.

CASE STUDY Island County

After the coalition wrote its vision statement, it came up with a list of almost 30 details, each representing a specific action item that had to be accomplished before the complete vision could be realized. Here are the first seven, just to give you an idea of how this part of the process works:

Island County's new Comprehensive Plan must

- *comply with the State's Growth Management Act;*
- *adopt standards for rural development that protect wetlands, streams, steep slopes, beaches, prime habitat, and other critical areas;*
- *adopt standards for rural development that keep densities and uses compatible with rural character;*

- adopt policies that help farmers and foresters make adequate livings on their lands;

- plan our cities, villages, crossroads, and residential communities to be pedestrian-oriented and people-friendly;

- provide for a mix of housing; and

- balance regulatory measures with non-regulatory options and incentives.

PLAY IT AGAIN

- Research your problem:

  - Find out if there are groups already organized to work on it.

  - Be skeptical, especially of people who tell you nothing can be done.

  - Be relentless in pursuing the information you need.

  - Use multiple sources.

  - Unearth the history of the problem.

  - Identify the stakeholders in this problem.

  - Learn the vocabulary of this problem and how it affects the discussion.

  - Listen to groups or individuals opposed to what you want to see happen.

  - Gain at least a beginner's handle on any technical background important to this problem.

  - Find out what's below the waterline—both hidden agendas and personal emotional baggage.

  - Don't be afraid to bail out, if at this early stage you find that this problem was not as much "your" problem as you'd thought. Find another problem to work on.

- Decide the form of your participation: you can join an existing organization or launch your own effort, either by yourself or by forming a group of your own.

- Create a specific project to address the problem you've chosen. Start by reviewing what you've learned about your problem. Discuss ideas with friends and potential allies. Determine the scope of your project—something not out of reach, but not too cautious either.

WHAT'S NEXT?

You've defined a project, created a vision for it, and come up with enough details to start planning in chapter 5. In the next chapter, we'll take a break from action steps and look at how trust and caring can help you make a difference in your community and the world.

- *Create a vision of your project's success. A vision is a mental picture of something that does not yet exist—a picture so clear and strong that it helps make that something real.*

- *Visions are important because of their power to inspire, to guide, and to keep organizations and groups focused and together.*

- *A vision must be clear and positive. It must be big enough. It must include changes in attitudes and a clear picture of your personal role. A vision comes from the heart, not the head—it is not the same as goals or objectives.*

- *Add details to your project. Creating a vision should have sparked some new thinking about your project.* What, exactly, does this project have to accomplish in order to make its vision real?

CHAPTER THREE

Wherever there is a human being, there
is an opportunity for kindness.
SENECA

---------------------------■---------------------------

TRUST *THEM?* ARE YOU KIDDING?

THE PUBLIC PROCESS solves problems best when people deliberate with respect, integrity, and concern for the common good.

But that conduct is not what we usually see in the public arena—at any level—and it's not the way most people think about any public process, especially where there's conflict or the possibility of conflict. From the U.S. Congress to your local school board, too often we see the public process bringing out the worst in people, not the best. Getting involved in it often seems as attractive as having a root canal.

That's a tragedy. As I said in the preface to this book, what most often separates success from failure in solving public problems is a positive and compassionate spirit, and competence in the so-called soft skills that flow from such a spirit—such as building trust, communicating with sensitivity, and inspiring others. What's in your heart is at least as important as what's in your head.

KEY POINT ■ *Being a successful agent for change is about more than making the right moves. It's also about making the moves right.*

The challenge is to develop and use the qualities of your own spirit that will help you solve tough problems in ways that build cooperation and community instead of pushing people further apart. This is easier said than done. I've seen too many brilliant analyst and otherwise competent managers fail because they couldn't or wouldn't do this.

WHAT'S YOUR EXPERIENCE? ■ *In your community, when's the last time you saw your school board, water district, town council, or county commission operate with "respect, integrity, and concern for the common good?" What difference did that make?*

THE IMPORTANCE OF BUILDING TRUST

The most important—and the most difficult to develop—quality of spirit in the public process is the ability and willingness to build trust, especially with opponents.

Whenever I talk about the importance of trust in solving public problems, I see eyeballs rolling up in the audience. "Sure, I'd like to trust," those eyes say, "but sometimes you just *can't* act that way in the Real World or you'll get run over. Where does this guy live, anyway? How smart is it to trust when the world is full of people who'll see it as a weakness to be exploited, and who can't wait to manipulate you and put you down?" Then I get the descriptions of crooked politicians, greedy CEOs, wacko neighbors, and beady-eyed bureaucrats. . . . Everyone seems to have someone like that in mind.

Yes, it's a tough world out there, with real villains in it. Yes, trusting is a risk—you can and probably will get hurt more than once. So what am I talking about?

Dealing with wars and revolutions and arms sales in the Foreign Service, I tangled with some of the worst people on the planet. I'm not naive about nasty people and the harm they can do, and I definitely don't underestimate the difficulty of dealing with them (but some of those people would have told you that I was no angel, either).

I started to change only when I realized, as a young diplomat at the United Nations, that a strategy of attacking and defending usually just led to escalating confrontations. At best, there were temporary "victories" that lasted as long as it took the other guys to lick their wounds and come back at me.

For me, it wasn't just foreign policy. My own first marriage was ending during the time I was at the UN, and the same lesson was just as evident at home. That marriage did not recover. But at the

UN, the efforts I made to build more trusting relationships with my counterparts began to bear fruit almost immediately.

<hr>

CASE STUDY At the United Nations

Trying to strengthen the arms embargo on South Africa (see chapter 1) was my first big test for using a more trusting approach at the United Nations. I never could have succeeded without the active cooperation of a half-dozen key diplomats from the Third World, all representing countries on the Security Council that had plenty of reasons not to trust the United States—or me. I was asking these people to persuade their superiors to put pressure on my own government to toughen the embargo, and they had every reason to think I had something up my sleeve. I had to convince them that what I was suggesting came from my genuine commitment to end apartheid. They had to trust me enough to take what was for all of them at least a modest bureaucratic risk. And, eventually, all of them took it.

That degree of trust didn't form overnight. In fact, when I arrived at the U.S. Mission to the United Nations in 1977, America's reputation throughout most of the Third World couldn't have been worse; my first challenge was just getting Third World diplomats to talk to me. It was no great leap to see that the honest dialogues the UN needed to solve the problems on its plate required trust, and that building trust meant taking the time, and caring enough, to put myself in other people's shoes and let them into mine.

I started by simply showing honest interest in other people's lives and sharing stories from my own. The diplomats were surprised at the openness, and some of them remained suspicious that this new openness from an American diplomat was another U.S. trick. But many more seemed willing to respond in kind. Slowly I began to build enough trust with some of the diplomats that we could begin to talk frankly about political problems.

Some months later, the Security Council passed the tougher arms embargo, made possible by the trusting relationships I'd built with my colleagues. When the committee I'd worked with gathered to celebrate, the chairman ordered the tape recorders turned off. After he'd congratulated everyone on the victory, he turned in my direction. "We all know the role Mr. Graham played," he said, "and we are very grateful." When I started to respond, a hand gently pushed me back in my seat, and the Zambian delegate sitting next to me described, with feeling, the personal impact on him of working with trust toward a common goal instead of the usual jockeying for national advantage. Three more Third World delegates followed him, saying essentially the same thing, and with a candor and emotion that I never heard in any UN session before or since. These feelings didn't disappear; in dealing with that one problem we created an atmosphere of at least modest trust that allowed us to approach other problems at the UN in a similar way. We weren't top dogs in our respective governments, so we didn't create world peace, but what we did made a difference and, I believe, inspired others.

HOW TO BUILD TRUST

My experience at the United Nations taught me lessons in building trust that I've used ever since.

Competence builds trust because it sets a standard. Both your allies and your opponents recognize your skills and experience; this makes miscalculations by any of them less likely and encourages straight talk. It also strengthens support for you from members of your own team. If they know how good you are at negotiating, for example, they'll be much more likely to trust you to take the lead at the bargaining table.

Accountability and *honesty* build trust; people know not only that you *can* do your job, but also that you *will* do it—and that you will tell the truth and keep your word.

Respect builds trust. Valuing other people's priorities, needs, backgrounds, outlooks, and styles helps them trust you, especially if they hold views that are very different from your own.

From my experience, however—

KEY POINT ■ *The most powerful tool for building trust is caring for other people and for their situations.*

By *caring* I don't mean some abstraction. Real caring is active—it goes past good thoughts to good actions, even when you're under stress. I apologize for spending the next section talking to you about what caring is—as if you didn't know that from your mother's knee. But I'm more than willing to embarrass myself because of the countless times I've seen citizen activists ignore the value of these simple steps.

■ A Caring Toolbox

Caring is putting yourself in others' shoes as best you can, so that you can more fully appreciate their feelings and needs. What must it be like to live this person's life? The more different that people are from you, the harder it is to do this, but it's very important that you try.

TRY THIS ■ *Think of a person who is opposing you on a problem—someone you find it really hard to care for. Ask yourself, what would it be like to be her/him? The next time you have to deal with that person, let those insights soften what you say and how you say it.*

Caring is minding all the little interactions. Who you are with the convenience store clerk is who you are.

TRY THIS ■ *The next time a telemarketer interrupts your dinner and you're tempted to give a rude response, consider that the caller may be a minimum-wage single mom or an overworked volunteer who has just had 15 people hang up on her. You can still say no, and you can still say, "Take me off your list," but spend another 10 seconds to add a few kind words that will make the person's tough evening a little brighter. Who knows what effect it might have?*

A GIRAFFE STORY
Steve Mariotti

When Steve Mariotti got mugged by teenagers on a New York City street, he didn't start agitating for better police protection. Instead, he started thinking of better ways for kids like the muggers to make a living. He had a hunch that streetwise kids could make it the way he had—by starting their own businesses. They were tough, assertive, and used to taking risks. What if the high energy levels some of these kids invested in illegal, destructive behavior could be channeled into legal entrepreneurship? Mariotti left his import-export business and became a business teacher in a ghetto high school.

To his greatest frustration, he found that "business" in the public schools meant typing and bookkeeping. The kids were bored and so was Mariotti. Again and again, he was told to stick to the text. Again and again he got fired for insisting that he had a better idea. "The system doesn't want real entrepreneurship," he says, "because it's so hard to control. Think about it—where else but school do they tell you which spot on the floor you can lay on for your naps? Entrepreneurs need to get out into the world and act."

Using his own savings, Mariotti set up the nonprofit National Foundation for Teaching Entrepreneurship. In 1985 he was finally hired by a principal who understood and supported his

Caring is looking for the positive. Acknowledge others for their strengths and contributions. Look for common interests and positive qualities rather than getting stuck on differences, weaknesses, and faults. Giraffe Steve Mariotti used the survival skills of street kids to turn them into successful entrepreneurs (see sidebar, page 40).

TRY THIS ■ *Think of people you really don't want to be around. Now think of something good about each of them—some character trait or skill, for example. Now think of things you might have in common—perhaps it's rooting for the same baseball team, perhaps something more. The next time you meet each person, find a way to acknowledge the good things and shared interests.*

Caring is being personal. It's getting to know people—sharing personal stories and experiences. This may mean being a little more open than you're comfortable with, and inviting others to respond in kind.

Caring is active, nonjudgmental listening. Caring communications aren't just about you talking.

WHAT'S YOUR EXPERIENCE? ■ *Think of a time, perhaps when you were feeling down, when someone really listened to you, not to tell you what was wrong with you but just to listen. What difference did that person's listening make for you? Have you ever listened that way to somebody else? What effect did it have?*

A GIRAFFE STORY
continued

program. That led to contracts with schools throughout the city. Five years later, the guy who got canned nine times was chosen High School Teacher of the Year by the national Federation of Independent Businesses.

Mariotti's students learn real-world skills like product development, marketing techniques, and financial planning. He takes classes on guided tours of New York's wholesale markets. The students each get a $50 grant to buy items that they then resell. Mariotti says this experience is "almost like a religious awakening . . . they'll never pay retail again."

Since 1985 Mariotti's students have started more than 45 new companies, ranging from chore services to rap-song writing. Mariotti sees them helping with the economic regeneration of their neighborhoods. "I'm trying to produce a community of merchants. The program isn't about making money. It's about making people's lives better."

As for himself, he says, "When I come home from working with these kids, I feel great. I never used to feel that good when I was just making money."

Web link: The National Foundation for Teaching Entrepreneurship (www.nfte.com).

Caring is doing small favors. I live down a long, winding dirt road that has 15 other families on it; some of them have always been friendly, some not. Visitors to all our houses are constantly getting lost, so I decided to make a detailed map showing how to reach all 16 houses. I gave copies to everyone on the road and to the firehouse and the county EMTs so that they could find us all, too. The next time I was out patching potholes, people who had never helped before came out with their shovels. There was a new friendly spirit, and I have no doubt that that little map helped cause it.

Caring is taking the time. No matter how rushed you are, there's always something caring you can do, even if it's only in the tone of your voice.

Caring is reaching out to people beyond your regular circle of family and friends.

Caring cannot be a manipulation. That will backfire, and you will end up much worse off than before.

Most of this stuff is small. Do it, however, and you might see a difficult person defrost. Trust, backed by genuine caring, permits dialogues that aren't possible any other way.

CASE STUDY The Everglades

A few years back I was asked to help design and lead a conference on the future of the Everglades. Environmentalists wanted the Everglades' natural flows restored. Sugar planters wanted to keep using fertilizers that leached into the groundwater. Developers in coastal cities wanted a cheap supply of drained land for new suburbs. Other people in the cities wanted to slow the flight to those suburbs to protect the tax base for urban schools. Dade County wanted to build a new airport in the swamp. The Army Corps of Engineers and local politicians all had their points of view. It was a swamp in more ways than one.

All the stakeholders came to Fort Lauderdale for this conference. I worked with the organizers to set up the agenda so that people from every group got to talk at length about who they were and why they wanted what they wanted. Nobody else had to agree—but they *did* have to listen. Then I led the group in a visioning exercise—what did they see for the Everglades in 2015? The effects of listening and of visioning—instead of the usual posturing by interest groups—were dramatic. Tentatively at first, then with more energy, people began to make suggestions that were genuinely aimed at finding common ground. They did that not because of changes in their own views or personalities, or in response to the eloquence of others. They did that because by then they'd begun to see each other as human beings with legitimate points of view, to care about each other's situations, and to build enough trust to permit the kind of openness (and open-mindedness) that could lead to real solutions.

■ The Personal Benefits of Caring Are Also Important

Remember the movie *Groundhog Day*? Bill Murray's character gets stuck in one day that's repeated over and over until he slowly, slooowly learns that caring produces meaning and happiness in his life and in the lives around him—instead of the discord and loneliness he had created by being cynical and manipulative. That movie made the case as well as it can be made.

EFFORTS TO BUILD TRUST ARE RISKY

The kind of cooperation achieved by the South Africa Arms Embargo Committee, and by the discussions on the Everglades, can happen when some trust has been established and is impossible without it. The story of how Giraffe John Hayes built enough trust to solve a serious land-use conflict is another good example (see sidebar, page 44). Trust gets established when people begin to care about each other and each other's situation as well as their own.

But you also need to remember the obvious: efforts at building trust, including initiatives of caring, are risky and don't always work. There are times when the people you're dealing with are too nasty or the situation is just too far gone to even try. Gandhi trusted that the British could eventually be persuaded to leave

India peacefully, and it worked; his tactics wouldn't have persuaded Hitler to leave Poland. I could take the risks of building trust with my fellow UN diplomats—but I never would have done so with Henry Kissinger, my boss under presidents Nixon and Ford; *trust* was not in his vocabulary.

TRY THIS ■ *When you're faced with the choice of trying to build trust or not, assess both the people and the situation you're dealing with. Initially you may come up with all the reasons not to trust: the situation is too tough or the opponent too nasty; there isn't enough time; you could be played for a chump. Now ask yourself whether you're making a true appraisal of the odds—or conning yourself so that you won't have to risk making the first trusting move. Remind yourself that building trust can bring important benefits despite the risks. Then make your decision.*

It's not all or nothing. You will rarely have enough information at the outset of a negotiation or confrontation to make a good appraisal of whether trust is possible. So it makes little sense to *start* with an attack-and-defend strategy. Navigate by positives unless and until it becomes clear that the other people will not do likewise. Give others the opportunity to respond in kind, and if they do, be prepared to build on that (see chapter 7). Meanwhile, take Wild Bill Hickok's advice: never sit with your back to the door. Make sure you've left yourself

A GIRAFFE STORY
John Hayes

John Hayes was raised in Aspen, Colorado, where he learned to love the land. Over time he became dismayed at the unplanned and uncontrolled development that was spoiling the area, and he began looking for a place in the world that was as special as Aspen had been when he was a boy. He discovered the Methow Valley in Washington State and moved there in the 1970s. Soon, however, he saw ugly, unplanned development threatening to destroy that paradise too. He vowed not to let that happen.

What he's done ever since for wildlife, water conservation, and the protection of open space in the Methow Valley has been extraordinary. He started a nonprofit corporation to preserve open space and wildlife habitat in the valley. He designed and built a 16-mile community trail system that links cross-country ski trails with backcountry trails and service facilities. He implemented a new approach to land use that preserves more than 90 percent of the land as open space for scenic, wildlife, and agricultural use. He's gotten water-conservation standards written into county rules, persuaded owners to hide their building sites in the trees, and worked closely with natural-resources agencies to protect wildlife areas.

Hayes's success in creating workable solutions to very

enough time, resources, and opportunity to defend yourself if and when it's clear that the only goal of *these* people is to flatten you.

I've noticed that most of the people who tell me that trusting in tough situations is naive haven't actually tried it. Well-considered efforts to build trust are *not* naive; in fact, my experience is that they consistently raise the odds for success. What's really naive is believing, despite so much evidence to the contrary, that the tired game of attacking and defending will somehow work next time around.

When you get right down to it, the biggest obstacle to a more trusting approach may not be a nasty opponent; it may be our own skepticism that such an approach can ever work. There have been times when I've stepped forward to build trust—and times I've run in the other direction when I shouldn't have. But in a lifetime of negotiating, when I've taken the risk to care and to try to build trust, the benefits have far exceeded the losses.

KEY POINT ■ *Successful citizen activism often depends on individual people and/or small groups sticking their necks out to trust when no one else seems ready to take that risk.*

In chapter 4 we'll discuss how building trust is essential to successful teams. In chapter 7 we'll look at how building trust can help you negotiate and resolve conflicts, and I'll give more examples.

A GIRAFFE STORY
continued

tough problems and age-old conflicts comes from more than hard work; it comes from bringing together people who often are in conflict—cattle ranchers, Native Americans, environmentalists, local and state bureaucrats and politicians, corporations, and land developers.

The trail project, for example, required that Hayes persuade owners along 16 miles of land to give up very valuable strips through their properties. If even one landowner had said no, the project would have been blocked.

Part of Hayes's success in bringing people together has been his ability to convey a vision for preserving the valley. He's become the "land preacher," and through his leadership he has raised the consciousness of everyone involved.

But perhaps most important has been Hayes's ability to earn the trust of virtually all the factions in the valley, a trust he earned through his strong sensitivity to the feelings of the many different people with whom he works. Hayes understands that bridging the distance between many opposing factions means addressing all their needs and satisfying people of very different backgrounds. He knows that this takes time, respect, caring, and patience, and John Hayes has given all that to saving the Methow.

PLAY IT AGAIN

WHAT'S NEXT?

It's not likely that you'll be able to do what you want to do, all on your own. The next chapter is about forming, motivating, and leading teams.

- Being a successful agent for change is about more than making all the right moves. It's also about making the moves right. A positive and compassionate spirit, and the interpersonal skills that flow from it, are important, practical elements of active citizenship.

- Making efforts to build trust with people—including opponents—very often helps solve problems and settle conflicts when nothing else will.

- Navigate by positives unless and until it becomes clear that the other people will not do likewise.

- The best way to build trust is through competency, accountability, honesty, respect, and—above all—caring. Caring is

  - putting yourself in others' shoes as best you can

  - minding all the little interactions

  - looking for the positive

  - being personal

  - active, nonjudgmental listening

  - doing small favors

  - taking the time

  - reaching out to people beyond your regular circle

  - not a manipulation

- The personal benefits of caring are important.

- Efforts at building trust entail risk, and they don't always work.

- When you're faced with the choice of trying to build trust or not, assess both the people and the situation you're dealing with. If you feel yourself backing away, ask yourself whether you're making a true appraisal of the odds—or conning yourself so that you won't have to risk making the first trusting move.

- Successful citizen activism often depends on individual people and/or small groups sticking their necks out to trust when no one else seems ready to take that risk.

*I am going to act and believe that if we all work together and
do our best, that something can happen. Not because I see it
happening, except in small ways, but because I know it can.*
PATCH ADAMS

BUILDING A TEAM AND
KEEPING IT TOGETHER

MOST OF THE public problems that cry for solutions today are complex and time-consuming. While change efforts are usually started by one or a few motivated people, long-term progress usually requires more than that. And it isn't just the additional help that's important. Given the power of the forces any citizen activist may confront, it's simply too easy for one person to be marginalized. If you're pursuing a cause by yourself, sooner or later those opposed to change are going to ask, if this is so important, why is she the only one making noise? Why don't we just ignore him?

But simply collecting a large number of willing people isn't enough. The work these people do has to be focused and coordinated. There has to be a *team*.

A team is more than a group of people sharing a common goal and working together to achieve it. A good team is an effective structure for planning, making decisions, coordinating efforts, and bringing power to bear. A good team is synergistic—members motivate each other, build on each other's strengths and compensate for weaknesses, share the heavy lifting, and cross-fertilize ideas.

Teams can be parts of larger groups, such as the committees of an organization or association, or they can be formed from scratch, to carry out new projects. Many of the functions and attributes of a team are also important for official or semiofficial bodies, such as planning commissions or citizens' advisory groups.

Teams are important, of course, in business and government, from IBM to NASA. Much of what's in this chapter is relevant to those worlds too.

HOW TO BUILD A TEAM FROM SCRATCH

The key is getting the right people.

■ Create the Core

The first step in building a team is to find a few people who enthusiastically share your motivation and mission, and whom you trust and get along well with. They become the core of the team, and their first job is to recruit the members of a larger team that will actually do the work. Team leadership at this stage is informal, and decisions are collegial. You may be the one who calls and chairs the initial meetings, but the longer-term leadership of the team is not a decision to be made at this stage.

USER'S GUIDE

The opening section of this chapter is about taking groups of people who share a common concern and turning them into teams. It's addressed principally to the citizen activist seeking to build a team around a new initiative, or to build a new committee or work team within an already established organization. If neither of these conditions applies to you, then you might want to skip this section.

If you *do* need to build a team, then apply what you need from this first section to fit your situation. If your effort is going to be large, long, and complex, then your team building will take time and effort. If all you want to do is round up a few of your buddies to help with a simple task, then what's here is overkill; your team building can be informal and minimal. Most projects are someplace in between.

■ Choose Team Members Carefully

It's assumed that by now you've got a good idea of the scope of the problem you're taking on and of the project needed to solve it. Now your core team needs to translate this information into an estimate of how many people—and what kinds of people—you need to help get the job done.

A good team can be more than the sum of its parts—but only if it has the right parts. Just filling the chairs is not enough. Include people representing a fair cross-section of any groups and organizations whose advice and support you know you will need. If your project has to do with combating violence or substance abuse in your children's school, for example, then teachers, administrators, parents, cops, and kids should be represented.

Include people with the skills, experience, and contacts you think the team will need. Does it need a lawyer, for example, or a publicist or someone with fund-raising experience? You wouldn't start a business enterprise with a key skill missing; the same reasoning applies to a volunteer project.

Begin your recruiting by approaching people who are already known to members of your core group, and who perhaps have already listened sympathetically to your concerns. It's unlikely, however, that you'll find the people with all the qualifications and contacts your team needs just in that initial circle of friends. Expand the search to people recommended by these friends, and then to others you think are likely to share your concerns about the problem. Finally, consider organizations, such as local service or cause groups, or local leadership development programs whose aims are close to yours; they might be sources of team members with the right affiliations and skills.

Steer clear of people whom you know from good experience are overly difficult to work with. Affiliation, skills, and experience aren't everything.

CASE STUDY Island County

Confronting the need to counter out-of-control development, those of us who started the Island County Citizens' Growth Management Coalition recruited part of our initial team from the five most active environmental groups in the county, as well as from two local chapters of statewide environmental groups that shared our concerns.

We focused our other recruiting efforts on people with the skills, experience, and contacts in areas important to solving our problem. For us, that meant research, environmental law, media, fund-raising, writing, and public speaking. We found all but one of those skills locally—we were not able to recruit an environmental lawyer, so we had to hire one in Seattle to help us shape our legal positions.

By carefully choosing our team, we not only greatly expanded our capabilities, but we also signaled to the opposition that we meant business, and almost overnight we became a formidable force in shaping county land-use policies.

TEAM STRUCTURE

Nobody wants more structure on a team than is necessary. If overdone, it stifles both energy and creativity. But the need for structure grows with the size and complexity of the work. It's crucial, early on, for the team to reach agreement on the five elements listed below, hopefully by consensus:

- leadership

- internal communications

- external communications

- decision making

- record keeping

The agreement doesn't have to be signed in blood, but it should be formally written down in some form of minutes or bylaws that all agree to. Not to address these elements invites conflict, inefficiencies, and chaos (see the case study on page 53).

■ Leadership

The question of *who* will lead the team is important. Even more important, however, is the *form* of leadership the team needs and wants.

KEY POINT ■ *The key concern any team must address head-on and early is how much authority it is comfortable giving to its leader.*

Will the leader's roles and responsibilities be limited to calling and chairing meetings? Or does it make sense in your

Brooklyn's East New York section used to be a good place to live. In 1967 Louise Stanley became a proud home owner there, working at the post office and raising her six children. But the area began to deteriorate, and after years of neglect, many buildings had been abandoned or even torched. Vacant lots had turned into trash heaps. Drug dealers were taking over the empty buildings. In a city where good, affordable housing is practically a myth, Louise Stanley couldn't stand seeing buildings empty.

Remembering when the neighborhood was friendly and open, she yearned to get rid of the criminals who had moved in. So Stanley attended a meeting of ACORN (the Association of Community Organizations for Reform Now). She'd gone intending to listen, but she soon found herself raising her hand, speaking her mind, and volunteering for assignments. A few weeks later she was leading the first East New York ACORN group.

Within two years Stanley and her ACORN group had organized a community of people to reclaim and renovate abandoned buildings in the neighborhood. Families moved into empty city-owned buildings. Neighbors provided power and water. Volunteers like Stanley worked with the families on rehabbing the buildings.

team's situation to give the leader broader powers to make decisions and to represent the entire team to others?

However much formal authority the team decides to give its leader, my experience is that it's important to allow the leader reasonable flexibility. In a crisis or other fast-breaking event, you should want your leader to have more authority to make decisions than in less stressed times—there simply may not be time to talk through all the options with the whole team. So the leader needs to be someone the team trusts to use and not abuse this privilege.

At this early stage, it's also important for the team to decide how leadership will be elected and how it can be changed, which includes setting terms of office.

Who will be the leader? Often it will seem natural and effective to choose as leader the spark plug who brought the core team together. But sometimes that person doesn't want the job, or there's consensus that somebody else on the team might be better suited. Sometimes, as in the case of Giraffe Louise Stanley, leadership emerges spontaneously (see sidebar, page 50). Unfortunately, given the time and effort that leadership requires, the question often comes down to who is *willing* to do the job. If that's the case, the best option may be to spread leadership responsibilities among several people who work well together.

■ Internal Communications

Good team communications are crucial—team members must have the information needed to do their jobs, including

A GIRAFFE STORY
continued

City Hall had the new residents arrested. Stanley, by then a savvy activist, was pleased. She alerted the press, and the resulting furor put the city on the defensive. Here were poor people fixing up abandoned apartments, and the city was arresting them?

Stanley negotiated with the city, and a deal was struck. ACORN agreed not to break into any more buildings. The city agreed to set up the Mutual Housing Authority of New York to give abandoned housing units to community groups for rehabilitation. The city also provided $2.7 million to buy renovation materials for 58 buildings. Not a bad result for a novice organizer. Stanley says, "The bottom line is getting people to realize that success is possible." That's leadership.

Louise Stanley had no idea she'd end up leading a movement that would reclaim a good hunk of East New York from urban decay. For her, as for many Giraffes, leadership "happened." When she found herself in the middle of an issue she cared a lot about, she rolled up her sleeves and went to work, becoming a leader along the way.

Web link: ACORN (www.acorn.org).

background facts, logistics data, and breaking news relevant to the team's work. They also need to know broadly what each other is doing, so that they can better coordinate the work.

The Internet is the quickest and most effective way for team members to communicate with each other.

TRY THIS ■ *Consider setting up a password-protected electronic bulletin board or newsgroup and then tasking team members to log on in a timely way, especially if the project is fast moving.*

■ External Communications

Who will speak for the team to outsiders, including the press? While the team as a whole may decide the policies that then need to be communicated, it's important to limit the number of people on the team who are authorized to deliver the message. This is not just to take advantage of your most articulate speakers, but it's also to minimize the chances of delivering mixed or contradictory messages.

■ Decisions

The team must agree on a clear, unambiguous process for making decisions: who gets to make them—and how? Consensus is a good goal to shoot for, but to avoid gridlock when consensus fails, set up a voting mechanism. Decide how many members of the team are needed to form a quorum, and how many votes are needed for approval. It's common to use majority rule for most decisions but to require a supermajority (60 percent, for example) for the most important ones—such as on spending a large amount of money, entering into a long-term contract, or initiating or joining a lawsuit.

Evelyn Schaeffer, who took on the phone company in Ohio (see chapter 2), offers the following tip for making team decisions. Frankly, I've never done it this way, but what she says makes sense: "The rock-bottom rule I never broke was to always ask after every decision, 'Is there anyone who can't live with this?' It's amazing how you can have an acrimonious split decision on something, but if you ask that question, the minority will usually say, 'I guess we can live with it,' and hostility is defused. Of course, if on rare occasions there is someone who says, 'I can't live with it,' then I go back to the drawing board with the caveat that if we reach the same decision, that person may have to bow out."

■ Record Keeping

Keep minutes that record attendance at every team meeting, accurately describe any decisions made, and give a balanced summary of the discussions. One option is to keep notes during the meeting on a flip chart where everybody can see them, and then to write up the minutes from these. However they are prepared, minutes should be sent out for approval as soon after a meeting as possible, while memories are fresh.

If you plan to raise and spend any money at all, create a separate bank account in the team's name. Never use your personal account to transact team business; that can create financial snarls and invite criticisms you don't need. Scrupulously record all transactions.

If you figure your team will be around for a while, you may want to incorporate in your state as a nonprofit corporation (see "Resources") and then apply to the Internal Revenue Service for tax-exempt status so that you can offer a tax deduction to the financial backers you will need. Try to find a lawyer who'll file the applications for free.

If you don't have your own nonprofit status and want to be able to offer tax deductions, often you can find a like-minded tax-exempt organization in your area that will let you, for a fee, operate (and receive tax-deductible gifts) under its legal umbrella.

AVOID THIS MISTAKE ■ *There's a strong temptation to avoid or delay creating the structure an organization needs because what the group is doing is so important, and it's moving so quickly that there just isn't time to "do all that paperwork." I know this mistake because I've made it myself. I finally learned better (see below).*

CASE STUDY Island County

When we formed the Island County Citizens' Growth Management Coalition, we knew that we represented interests and approaches on land use and environmental protection that went from far left to center. When we took on the entrenched Island County commissioners over land-use policies, the situation was so pressing that our individual differences were quickly buried and we had no problem coming up with a shared vision for our work and with an overall strategy for what to do and how to do it. We operated well within a loose, informal framework with a decision-making process that was murky at best.

The problems came when we started winning, and the do-or-die tensions of our fight with the county lessened. As we sought to fine-tune our successes, individual differences among the coalition's members and member groups became more and more prominent—and we had virtually no structure to deal with them. Bruised by months of internal wrangling, the coalition finally had the sense to step back and spend two months producing a set of operating procedures we should have produced two and a half years earlier. By skipping this key step in our haste to deal with a crisis, we'd ended up almost imploding just as victory was in sight.

TEAM MANAGEMENT

The most important and most difficult aspect of managing a team is dealing with the people on it.

▪ Focus on Relationships

How people get along can be crucial to the success of any team effort, especially if the task you've taken on includes stress-producing conflicts or obstacles. The minimum goal is to create working relationships good enough to promote open discussion and ready cooperation.

If all the members of your group don't know each other at the outset, spend whatever time it takes at the first meeting—or set aside a special time—for everyone to get acquainted. Suggest that people share not just the usual biographical information but also the reasons why they're there, and whatever expectations, concerns, and questions they may have. As the project goes on, regularly schedule "people" time—pizza out, a ball game, a potluck with the kids, a celebration for a job well done—anything that brings team members together in an atmosphere that's informal and relaxed. If you've got the time and resources, a team retreat can help deepen connections.

KEY POINT ■ *It's important that members be as comfortable with each other as possible. But it's even more important that they trust each other to contribute to the work of the team.*

Chapter 3 focused on building trust with opponents or potential opponents. It's also vital to build trust among the people on your side. Mutual trust keeps a team motivated and moving forward. It improves coordination and communication. It makes the work more fun. It helps the team weather obstacles and disappointments.

Trust also provides a healthy framework for dissent, so that contrary opinions are given fair hearing. Good teams are never made up of robots, and the team vision, strategies, and goals are products of contributions, discussions, and even arguments. Members of a good team trust each other enough that when they *do* disagree, it's in the context of a shared commitment that holds them together even in dissent.

The ultimate goal is to create a team bond that allows many people to move almost as one; individual needs and priorities are not forgotten, but they're willingly subordinated to those of the team. That level of bonding is an ideal. Certainly it isn't always possible, but when it does happen, a team can be an almost magical enterprise, making the total effort of its members more than the sum of what each of them could do alone.

Chapter 3 suggested ways of building trust. *Competence* counts; if everyone on the team is qualified to act on the problem you've taken on, you're going to trust each other more to make a useful contribution than if you were all beginners. You can increase competence on your team by making sure that everybody has the information and training they need. Taking extra time in the beginning for this prep work will pay rich dividends when your project is in full swing and there's no time to stop for remedial training.

Accountability and *honesty* build trust—knowing that your teammates will do their jobs, especially when things get tough, and that they will tell you the truth, even when that might be difficult.

Respect for teammates' differing backgrounds, priorities, needs, and styles is important, too—especially if any of those elements in a teammate make you uncomfortable.

But, as mentioned earlier, the critical factor in building trust is *caring*. Working on a team whose members care for each other not only makes the work more enjoyable, but it also builds the trust within each person that the others appreciate and will act for the good of the group and its mission. Uncaring or selfish behavior has the opposite effect; teammates are reluctant to trust anyone they see acting only in his own interests, even on small things; they fear that in a crunch he'll just take care of himself. That view could make a difference in how the team performs, especially if it suddenly has to deal with a stressful issue.

WHAT'S YOUR EXPERIENCE? ■
Ever been on a team with someone who seemed constantly focused on her own needs, never going out of her way to help others? What about the opposite experience of working with someone who was always helpful— doing small favors, for example? How did these different attitudes affect the trust you and others put in these people? How comfortable were you working with each of them? Was there any effect on how the team performed?

Find ways to encourage caring actions on your team, and model them yourself. If you've got loners along who want to stay that way, that's fine. But every team member can be encouraged to share personal stories, listen to others, do small favors, and honestly share concerns. All of it helps. Others pick up on these examples, and as they do, trust expands among the entire team.

A GIRAFFE STORY
Global Volunteers

Global Volunteers has been called a "mom-and-pop Peace Corps." That makes Michele Gran "Mom" and her husband, Bud Philbrook, "Pop." Indeed, the idea for Global Volunteers was conceived on their honeymoon.

The couple, who lived in St. Paul, Minnesota, were already booked for a honeymoon cruise when Gran had a change of heart. She wanted a more meaningful beginning together. Philbrook had participated several years earlier in a community-development project in India, and he knew of a similar one in Guatemala, so the couple spent their first week of married life in a Guatemalan hut, working all day on community projects. When they returned to St. Paul, they found that—thanks to a newspaper article about their unusual honeymoon— other people wanted to know about traveling to serve. "People were coming up to me and saying, 'I've always wanted to do something like that, but the Peace Corps is too long a commitment,'" says Philbrook.

Philbrook, an attorney and former state representative, and Gran, who holds a master's degree in international communications, decided to bring average people together to do cross-cultural community development around the world. Global Volunteers was born.

The nonprofit organization recruits North American

■ Match the Right People with the Right Tasks

What people volunteer to do will often be a good guide, although of course it's also important to make sure that each person has the skills and experience needed to do the job. Matching new people with more experienced people on the team both ensures the quality of the work and provides on-the-job training. That's how the Giraffe organization Global Volunteers does it (see sidebar, page 56).

TRY THIS ■ *It's useful for team members early on to talk to the whole team about what they see as their primary strengths and interests. This not only helps guide the distribution of tasks, but it also makes each person feel valued, it will prompt shy members to contribute, and it will help the more compulsive members to relax, knowing that they don't have to know or do everything.*

If you're leading a team, try to rotate the toughest and most time-consuming jobs within the group to give people breathers when they need them. Also, delegate authority to others as much as you can. Delegating not only takes some of the load off the leader, but it also builds teamwork: when people know they're integral to the action, their commitment to the enterprise and to the team grows.

AVOID THIS MISTAKE ■ *Delegate authority only when it's clear that the person you're delegating to has the necessary skills and commitment. Don't ask the most*

A GIRAFFE STORY
continued

volunteers, who pay their own travel and living costs to work a few weeks far from home. U.S. volunteers don't show up and start directing the action; they join teams directed by community leaders. Gran and Philbrook explain to volunteers that they're going to work with and learn from their hosts, as a one-person-at-a-time way of waging peace. Much of Gran and Philbrook's work is in identifying communities that can use help and working with the communities' leadership.

Supported entirely by Gran and Philbrook, Global Volunteers operated in the red for years. The couple has faced bankruptcy more than once; their home has been collateral for the organization's credit rating. While they've coped with economic worries, Philbrook and Gran have also had to contend with the opinion of some foreign aid professionals that they were "idealists stuck in the '60s."

Undaunted, Gran and Philbrook are waging peace today with as much passion and conviction as ever. With Global Volunteers now in its 20th year, it's gone from one project that sent 9 volunteers to Jamaica, to mobilizing more than 13,500 volunteers on community-development projects worldwide, touching hearts and changing lives in 20 countries.

Web link: Global Volunteers (www.globalvolunteers.org).

tongue-tied member of your team, for example, to sub for you in giving a speech to the city council.

▪ Recognize and Act Early on Potential Problems within the Team

Spend enough time at your first team meeting making sure that everybody understands what he or she is getting into. A brief review is good insurance. It's like when the pilot announces your destination before they close the main cabin door. I've yet to see some red-faced soul bolt for the door—but I'm sure it's happened.

Especially if you're in a position of leadership, be on the lookout for the kinds of little frictions and mistakes on your team that can grow into big trouble later on. Is any team member weaker in needed skills than you thought? Are those snide remarks between Terry and Jerry going to build into a nasty fight just when you need people to pull together? Could Simon's gung-ho optimism lead him to underestimate risks?

If you're alert for warning signs like these, you or other members of the team can take preemptive actions that will reduce the chances for real problems later on. You might, for example, reassign responsibilities among team members, try to mediate disputes before they get out of hand, or offer a private word of coaching or advice. You may not end the problems, but by addressing them early, you and the team will at least have a better chance to lessen them and/or compensate for their effects.

CREATE AND COMMUNICATE A TEAM VISION OF SUCCESS

Chapter 2 described why visions are important and how to create one. Visions are especially important for teams—there's a special synergy generated when all team members have put their pictures of intended results into a single vision of what they'll achieve together. Teams that don't have a common vision, or whose vision is mushy or incomplete, are more likely to bog down in confusion and conflicts over problems that should be minor.

Your team will work harder and better if it's guided by a vision that all members have helped create. As members contribute to a team vision—each adding his or her own pictures of success—the vision tends to get stronger and clearer; individuals increase both their sense of responsibility for it and their commitment to attaining it.

Use the visioning exercise described in the section "What's the Vision for Your Project?" in chapter 2 with the team. If you're leading the exercise, remind everyone that visions are intuitive, not intellectual: to create a vision, team members must give themselves the freedom to imagine what does not yet exist. Urge team members to add to or refine what others have said, and to contribute new pictures. Combine and condense the pictures into a short vision statement that will guide the team's subsequent planning (see chapter 5).

Getting team members to be visionaries isn't always easy. Some people have never seen themselves in that role and aren't comfortable with it. If it helps them to relax into it, don't use the word *vision* at all—simply ask people to join you in creating "pictures" of what the team wants to achieve: "What does it look like when we're done?"

You may have to get things started by describing your own pictures of what's to come. Make those pictures so clear and so compelling that your listeners are drawn into them and can see what you see, hear what you hear, feel what you feel. Communicating your vision this way not only creates a model, but it also encourages people who might otherwise be reluctant to be visionaries, too. Many people will overcome their hesitations when they see you going first. And once into it, they'll start to feel the same excitement you do, and the process can take off.

Some team members may be so impatient to "get on with the important questions" of strategies and tactics that they will want to roll right by the vision-setting process, especially if time is short. Resist that temptation and you'll save much frustration and disappointment down the line. Assure the impatient ones that setting goals and strategies is the next step in the planning process.

KEY POINT ■ *Successful teams make the investment of time and energy to develop a shared vision, one that's both a guide for planning and a source of energy and cohesion.*

PLAY IT AGAIN

WHAT'S NEXT?
You'll be in a mess without a good plan. Chapter 5 shows you how to create a plan to carry out your project, and how to put that plan into action.

- *A good team is an effective structure for planning, making decisions, coordinating efforts, and bringing power to bear. A good team is synergistic—members motivate each other, build on each other's strengths and compensate for weaknesses, share the heavy lifting, and cross-fertilize ideas.*

- *The first step in building a team is to find a few people who enthusiastically share your motivation and mission, and whom you trust and get along well with. They become the core of the team, and their first job is to recruit the members of a larger team that will actually do the work.*

- *Choose team members carefully. Include people representing a fair cross-section of any groups and organizations whose advice and support you know you will need. Include people with the skills, experience, and contacts the team will need to reach its goals.*

- *It's crucial, early on, for the team to reach agreement on the following:*

  - Leadership. *What's important is not just who will lead the team but also the form of leadership the team needs and wants.*

  - Internal communications. *Team members must have the information needed to do their jobs, including background facts, logistics data, and breaking news relevant to the team's work.*

  - External communications. *Who will speak for the team to outsiders, including the press?*

  - Decisions. *The team must agree on a clear, unambiguous process for making decisions: who gets to make them, and how?*

  - Record keeping. *Keep accurate minutes of meetings. Scrupulously record all financial transactions.*

- *Focus on relationships. How people get along can often be crucial to the success of any team effort.*

- *It's important that team members trust each other to contribute to team goals. Competence, accountability, honesty, and respect help build trust within a team, but the crucial factor is caring for the people you're with.*

- *Match the right people with the right tasks. If you're leading, delegate authority to others as much as you can.*

- *Recognize and act on potential problems within the team early.*

- *Create and communicate a team vision of success.*

CHAPTER FIVE

Visions are fine—but they must grow corn.
SUN BEAR

■

MAKING A PLAN

USER'S GUIDE

This chapter is addressed to a team of activists. The information here, however, works equally well if you are on your own.

I'M ASSUMING that you've identified a problem and created a project. You've formed a vision of the results you want. Now what?

Visions are about *what* you want. What's still missing is *how* to get it. Visions are the engine; action is the drivetrain.

AVOID THIS MISTAKE ■ *A vision that remains only a concept can do more harm than good, by raising expectations that will never be fulfilled.*

This chapter is about making a vision real by creating a plan for its fulfillment and putting that plan into action.

A good plan, effectively carried out, will keep your team organized and focused, help it make the most of its time and energy, and definitely improve its odds of getting the results it wants. Giraffes Mimi Silbert and Fred Mednick (see sidebars, pages 62 and 72), for example, created highly sophisticated projects that could not have succeeded without sound and detailed planning.

A good plan will also give your team standards it can use to evaluate results—to see where it succeeded and where it didn't, what it could have done better, and what it didn't need to do at all. This kind of analysis will make your team that much better prepared for its next project.

Have you ever worked on an activity or project in which nobody seemed to be handling the details or anticipating the next steps? What happened? How did you feel about it?

I call the planning method described below *visionary planning* because everything in it is tied to the overall vision of success you've created for your project. That link allows the power of the team's vision to inspire all its members, and the clarity of the team's vision to guide them, every step of the way.

STEPS FOR VISIONARY PLANNING

The steps described in this section are essentially the same no matter what the size of your project. They work whether you're planning a PTA fund-raiser or saving an old-growth forest.

■ Review Your Problem, Project, and Vision, and the List of Details You've Created So Far

If it all still seems right, continue. If not, fix the parts that seem "off."

■ Expand and Deepen the Research You've Already Begun

By now you should have a pretty good understanding of the challenge you've taken up. Your team's task from now on is to keep your research at least one step ahead of the decisions you have to make. Since the decisions tend to get more and

---

Mimi Silbert

Not many people choose to spend their lives working with convicted felons and drug addicts. But Mimi Silbert, founder of San Francisco's Delancey Street rehabilitation project, has committed her every waking hour to helping ex-cons become productive, welcome members of society.

Silbert knows what gets results: Since the program began, Delancey Street has rescued more than 11,000 former convicts, addicts, prostitutes, and alcoholics, without government funding. The foundation has grown to include 25 commercial enterprises run by 500 recovering addicts and convicts working out of a $30 million residential/ business complex on San Francisco's waterfront. Taken together, Delancey Street's enterprises generate enough revenue to keep the foundation fully self-sufficient.

Silbert could have taken her formidable skills anywhere. But she cites her solid family upbringing as the reason she chooses to stick her neck out for the common good: "Delancey Street functions the way my own family did—everybody looked out for everybody else as we struggled upward. That's what happens here every day. Together we rise or fall."

Silbert's approach is simple. Incoming Delancey Street residents must learn three different trades and take part in weekly group sessions that

more detailed as a project proceeds, so must the research. Examples:

- *In your initial research, you might have determined that you need the support of the mayor's office. As your plan starts to take shape, you may now need to know precisely which official in the mayor's office can offer the help you need—and is most likely to give it.*

- *For starters, you may have researched the media outlets that can best help you get the word out about your project. As you begin to implement the media options in your plan, you'll need to know contact names and numbers, press deadlines, and so on (see chapter 9).*

- *You might have mastered what at first you thought were all the technical details you needed to know. Now you discover that you've just opened the door to even more complicated problems that also bear on your project.*

■ Identify the Obstacles, Risks, and Resources That Impact Your Project

Write down in a column on a flip chart every *obstacle* and *risk* for your project that you can think of. If you looked at potential obstacles when you created a vision for your project (see "What's the Vision for Your Project" in chapter 2), include them here. Now have your team brainstorm all the *resources* it can see—the people, things, attitudes, laws, influences, and so on— that can help it overcome the obstacles and risks. The time, talent, and enthusiasm you and your team members can spend on the project are key resources. Write these resources down in another column.

promote self-understanding, interpersonal communication, and basic life skills. And no one leaves without the equivalent of a high school diploma.

Despite daunting national statistics on recidivism among ex-convicts, Silbert starts with the assumption that people can change, and, from there, she helps them create that change. "We have a saying, 'to act as if,'" Silbert explains. "We say if you walk around saying 'please' and 'thank you,' you will become a person who talks that way naturally. And if you act as if you believe in yourself, you will."

For Silbert, Delancey Street remains a work in progress, mirroring the lives of her "clients." The foundation's construction projects provide a case in point: "You're building your own foundation here. If you make a mistake with a wall or a joint, you tear it down and rebuild it. That's what we're doing here at Delancey Street for ourselves— tearing down bad crooked things and replacing them with good straight things."

In a world where most convicted criminal offenders and hard-core drug addicts emerge from prison and from treatment programs unchanged, Silbert wants to spread the Delancey Street success: "Our biggest issue now is to replicate this model. You need a strong, visionary, committed lunatic to dedicate a life to initiate

Island County

Initially, the Citizens' Growth Management Coalition saw the following obstacles, risks, and resources:

something. But to continue, Delancey Street must be bigger than I am."

Web link: The Delancey Street Foundation (www. eisenhowerfoundation.org/ grassroots/delancey/index. htm).

■ **Obstacles and Risks**

▓ *unanimous opposition from the County Board of Commissioners*

▓ *no money*

▓ *not enough volunteers*

▓ *an extremely complicated task and not enough information*

▓ *public ignorance and apathy*

▓ *expensive lawsuits we could lose; personal legal liabilities*

▓ *personal impact of too much time spent away from livelihoods and families*

▓ *conflicts with developers and property-rights advocates that could get nasty*

■ **Resources**

▓ *legal advantage: the State Growth Management Act favored our side*

▓ *a community that we thought could be energized, once given the information*

▓ *a number of skilled and committed people at the core of the effort*

▓ *rapid internal communications via the Internet*

▓ *research made much easier by the Web*

▓ *connections to other activist groups in other counties*

■ **Brainstorm Possible Solutions**

Look at the column of obstacles and risks, and see how many of them you can lessen or eliminate with the resources you've identified. Draw these links on the flip-chart page as possible solutions. If you looked at potential obstacles when you created a vision for your project, remember the solutions you came up with in that exercise, and write them in on the flip chart, too.

In the Island County case, for example, legal obstacles and risks were softened by the fact that the state's new growth management law seemed to be on the coalition's side. Lack of money and volunteers could be overcome by soliciting money and public support in our community. The Web would make our research much easier.

Continue searching for links between obstacles/risks and resources, and brainstorming possible solutions—don't limit yourself to the resources you've already identified. Fill up the page with solutions. Fill up several pages. The purpose is not just to catalyze your thinking—it's also to build your confidence and enthusiasm that the task you've taken on can be done and that its vision can be realized.

■ Create an Action Plan

An *action plan* is what you use to keep you on course and on schedule as you work on your project. Here's how to create an action plan:

Write the name of your project and your vision for its success at the top of a very large sheet of paper. Butcher paper works, as do several flip-chart pages taped together.

Draw a horizontal timeline across the top of the paper, just under the vision. Put today's date on the far left of that line. On the far right, write the date on which you expect your project to be completely and successfully finished.

Break down your project into goals. I use the word *goal* in this book to describe an aim or objective essential to the success of the project you've taken on. A complex project might have six or more goals. Taken together, the goals, when achieved, represent the completion of the entire project and the realization of your vision. *The goals add up to the vision.*

A good way to come up with the goals for your project is to look at

■ *the details you've already described for your project;*

■ *the obstacles, risks, and resources you've identified;*

■ *the possible solutions you've brainstormed.*

If you know that your project will require money to cover expenses, for example, then one goal will be to determine how much money you need, and to raise it. If swaying public opinion will be important to the success of your project, then another goal will be to build that support by creating and carrying out a successful media strategy (see chapter 9).

Make sure that the goals you come up with do all the work needed to complete the project, without duplicating efforts.

List the goals down the left side of your action plan as in the example below, leaving plenty of space between them.

While we didn't write it down quite this way, here's what the action plan for the Citizens' Coalition might have looked like at this stage:

CASE STUDY Island County

CITIZENS' GROWTH MANAGEMENT COALITION ACTION PLAN
Smart Growth for Island County

Vision

Island County remains a rural oasis in the crowded Puget Sound area. Its growth is managed by a Comprehensive Plan that meets state law, and it is a model for other rural places fighting to curb overdevelopment and sprawl.

TIMELINE

Project starts   Project ends
9/1/97 ■━━━━━━━━━━━━━━━━━━━━━■ 12/31/01

Goals

Legislative. Research, prepare, and deliver policy papers that influence each aspect of the county's draft Comprehensive Plan as it comes before the Planning Commission and Board of Commissioners.

Negotiating. Negotiate mutually acceptable solutions to each contested point as far as possible.

Litigating. Successfully litigate problems that cannot be successfully negotiated.

Public education. Build broad-based public support for the coalition's positions by creating and carrying out a successful media strategy.

Electoral. Find, support, and elect candidates for the County Commission who are more favorable to the coalition's views.

Funding. Determine, and raise, the amount of money needed to carry out this project.

Tighten the focus of your plan by breaking down each goal into smaller and more specific parts. Goals point the way to the desired ends, but for them to serve as planning guidance, you need something more specific. Start by breaking down each goal into the *steps* needed to achieve it. For example, if a goal is to raise money, then the steps toward that goal might include the following:

- *Create a budget.*
- *Develop a mailing list of possible donors.*
- *Write and send out a direct-mail piece to possible donors.*
- *Organize and carry out visits to potential major donors.*
- *Research possibilities for foundation funding; write and send proposals.*

Cross-check every item you want to put into your plan with your vision: if a suggested goal or step doesn't help you get to the vision, it doesn't belong in the plan—or the vision needs to be adjusted so that it does.

Write the steps underneath each goal. Now draw a horizontal timeline underneath each step. Put the right end of the timeline on the day when you know that step has to be finished if the goal it serves is to be achieved on time. Estimate how long that step will take to carry out. Using that information, *count backward to the day when work on that step must start*—that's the left end of the timeline (see the model on the next page).

When you've finished writing in the steps for the entire project, coordinate the timelines to make sure any actions that must be completed before others can start are done on time. For example, you can't visit potential major donors until you know who they are. Fund-raising has to be launched before you can spend the money.

Now write in *benchmarks* on each timeline to note specific events or accomplishments for that step. For example, if a step is "Organize and carry out visits to potential major donors," then benchmarks might note when 5 visits have been made, then 10, and so on. Determine the most distant benchmarks first, and then work backward in time. Some small steps may have no benchmarks other than the completion of the step.

Finally, work out with your team who takes responsibility for completing each of the steps. With a little patience, you can match most steps with people interested in working on them. If there's a specific job or two that nobody wants to do, draw straws or have people take turns.

After each step, write the name of the person or persons responsible for its completion.

Here's how all this might look on your action plan for just one goal and for just the first few months of a longer project. (Now you know why I said to start with a *very* big piece of paper!)

SAMPLE ACTION PLAN
Building a New Library in Plainsville

Vision

There's a new library in Plainsville, at the corner of Main and 2nd. People of all ages use it. It's a great resource and gathering place for the entire community.

TIMELINE

Project Starts   Project Ends

9/1/05   12/31/08

■━━━━━━━━━━━━━━━━━━━━━━━━━━━━┥ ┝━━━━■

Goals

1. _____

2. _____

3. Funding: Determine, and raise, the amount of money needed to carry out this project.

Steps

■ *Create a budget* (JOHN, ANN)

9/1/05   10/1/05

        FINISH

■ *Develop a list of potential donors* (MARK, SHARON, ROB)

9/1/05   11/1/05

■————————————————■

           FINISH

■ *Write and send out a direct-mail piece* (CARL, KARYN, KEITH)

    10/1/05   12/10/05

   ■————————————————■

            SENT

■ *Plan and carry out visits to potential major donors* (JOHN, ANN, KEITH)

    11/1/05   12/10/05 1/31/06   3/15/06

    ■————————■————————■————————■

         5 VISITS 10 VISITS 20 VISITS

■ *Research possibilities for foundation funding; write, and send proposals*
(MARK, JERRY, CHRISTINE)

  9/15/05   11/10/05   12/31/05   3/15/06

  ■————————————■————————————■————————————————■

         5 SENT   10 SENT   15 SENT

Create a budget. If your project requires money, then the funding goal in your action plan must be based on a budget, as in estimated expenses matched against estimated sources of cash income. Here's a stunner: unless you're the federal government, the cash income must equal or exceed the expenses. A budget should also list items given to you (*in-kind contributions*).

All foundations and many major donors will ask to see a budget before they write you a check, so be thoughtful in developing one. Make sure that all cost and revenue items are included, and that you can justify the type and amount of each. Be impeccable in handling the project's money (see "Record Keeping" in chapter 4, page 53).

AVOID THIS MISTAKE ■ *Good plans are carefully and thoroughly drawn, but no plan should ever be cast in concrete; the planning process needs to be open and flexible enough to respond to changing circumstances and new information. Don't wait until the problems or crises find you! Keep your positive attitude and vision, but spend enough time anticipating what might go wrong and then figure out what you might do to prevent it, or to cope with it if it can't be prevented. Keep these contingency plans handy, so that they're within reach when you need them.*

Be just as prepared to welcome the *good* breaks, and to expand your goals and vision in ways you could not possibly have envisaged when you started.

CASE STUDY **Ashtabula County, Ohio**

When Evelyn Schaeffer's group started its crusade in late 1993, its vision was the elimination of long distance tolls for all telephone calls made within Ashtabula County. At that time the Internet was almost unheard of, and there were no Internet service providers (ISPs) in the entire county.

Schaeffer's group never did fully eliminate long distance tolls within the county, but it *did* succeed in getting the county's four phone companies to eliminate long distance tolls for all calls made to the county seat. The effect of this was to let the emerging ISPs in the county seat offer flat-rate dial-up access for all county exchanges—permitting much quicker, easier, and cheaper access to the Internet for everybody. Schaeffer's group achieved its goal of countywide toll-free communication in a way it couldn't have predicted at the beginning.

Assess progress as you go. As the work proceeds, it's important that you regularly assess progress, evaluate your plan for discrepancies and overlaps, discuss solutions to problems, and make any necessary course corrections. If you're working in a team, the best way to assess is in regular team meetings. Use questions such as these:

- *Is the work on each step going forward on schedule?*
- *What problems or obstacles need to be dealt with now?*
- *Are we each completing the work we signed up to do?*
- *Do any of the work assignments need to be adjusted?*
- *Does everything we're doing serve our vision? If not, what adjustments need to be made? Does the action plan need to be changed in any way? Does the vision need changing? Perhaps it's become too small.*

Spend some time on more personal questions, such as these:

- *Is the project so far easier or harder than we thought it would be? Why?*
- *Are we being as bold, street-smart, and creative as we need to be? Are we using our intuition as well as our brains? Are we taking maximum advantage of new thinking and new technologies?*
- *Have there been unexpected events or lessons? What were they? How have we reacted to them?*

TRY THIS ■ *If at any point your effort seems to be losing momentum, stopping, going backward, or heading off in too many directions, bring it back on course by reviewing your vision as a team. Recall the pictures you developed in creating that vision, and rekindle their power to guide, to inspire, and to keep your group together.*

Assessment meetings are also a good time to bring in outside resources for any additional training or guidance your team might need. For example, you could invite a friend from a PR firm to coach the team on how to get media attention.

WHAT TO DO WHEN YOUR PLAN SUCCEEDS

Your project is completed, and you've made a difference in solving the problem that led you to launch it. But you're not done. Now's the time to celebrate—and to follow up on what you've accomplished.

■ Celebrate Your Success!

KEY POINT ■ *Celebrating the fruits of active citizenship should be more than just popping a bottle of champagne or taking the team out to a good restaurant when the job is done. To me, it's about reaffirming those qualities of the human spirit that say yes to challenge, that lead us to create, to care, to persevere no matter what the odds.*

Celebrating success can also keep you from slipping into a common pitfall for citizen activists: After a tough challenge has been met, it's too easy to remember just what the mountain looked like from the bottom. Too easy just to talk about whatever struggle and pain there might have been, or the faults of some tough characters you had to deal with along the way.

I've also come to see that celebrating is the grease that helps keep the creative process going. After a success, don't just keep your nose to the computer screen, doing business as usual. If you do that, the mental machinery that kept you creating starts to run out of tune, even starts to rust. So you're less likely and less able to tackle the next opportunity to create.

He's the man Jane Goodall calls "my little brother." But that's about the only "little" that can be applied to Fred Mednick—a man with big ideas, global vision, and super-sized energy. "Some people do extreme sports," he says. "I run an extreme nonprofit."

Mednick was headmaster of a prestigious private school and working on his Ph.D. dissertation when he had some realizations that changed his life. "So I fired myself," he's fond of saying, and, in June 2000, Teachers Without Borders (TWB) was born.

Mednick's dissertation research included surveying teachers worldwide. "They were writing great stuff," he says. "And the more I researched, the more I knew they needed access to each other and to information." When he learned there were 59 million of them—the world's largest grouping of professionally trained people—his dissertation's focus became their potential role as catalysts for community development. His life's mission became finding a way to foster that role for the world's teachers.

TWB's members are teachers and volunteers in 84 countries, and it relies on local partnerships to create programs that are relevant, sustainable, and invited in by the community. The organization works with teachers, students,

My experience also is that creative people get on a roll—each success seems to make the next one easier, and big successes seem to follow an appreciation of smaller ones. Celebrating is a way to keep the dice hot, to keep the magic going. To switch metaphors, imagine that celebrating success is pump priming—say thanks for every trickle and a real stream can follow.

Still, I know plenty of hard-working activists who find it hard to celebrate success. "Oh, it was nothing," they say, downgrading their achievements and not celebrating because they feel they shouldn't blow their own horns.

I think that's false modesty. Celebrating doesn't mean bragging. It means acknowledging a creative process that anyone can tap in to, but that few do. Think how easy it would have been for you to ignore the problem you solved, to have stayed out of it and let others do the work. Most of the world operates that way. You didn't. That makes you a role model for everybody else. Hooray for you!

■ Follow Up and Follow Through

After all the hard planning and work you've done, don't just walk off the field when you reach your goals.

KEY POINT ■ *Public policy is a dynamic process, and some backsliding in even the best of solutions is inevitable.*

You and your group need to monitor progress, keep the community informed, and make sure that agreed-upon policies

and communities, primarily in developing nations. Key TWB programs are teacher training and helping teachers worldwide connect with each other to share ideas and experiences. An online Certificate of Teaching Mastery was launched recently, its e-learning platform donated by Cisco Systems. The program gathers teachers from around the world in small cohorts. They learn from each other and also post their work to an electronic portfolio available for public viewing.

One of TWB's flagship programs is building Community Teaching & Learning Centers (CTLCs). These are as varied as the needs of the local residents they serve. Typically, they include an "online," computer-equipped room and an "offline" community gathering space. CTLC programs can include preschools, HIV/AIDS training, literacy, and mentorship. They sometimes also serve as cybercafes, health clinics, or crafts workshops.

Funded by grants and individual donors, TWB also secures corporate sponsorships, such as free shipping from DHL, a global shipping company that sends donated computers to their recipients. One of TWB's unanticipated outcomes has been the bridging of cross-cultural divides, even in high-conflict areas. In the course of Mednick's work with teachers, are enforced. It's fine to say that some government agency should be doing all that, but often those agencies need some friendly shoves.

Your solution will not have been perfect. Also, unforeseen circumstances and unintended consequences may arise. One way or the other, refinements will be needed over time, and you want to be at the table to keep your hard-won solutions pointed in the right direction.

■ Be Mindful of Your Legacy

The strategies and tactics you and your team have developed, the tone and attitudes you've modeled, and the relationships you've formed can all be used to help tackle similar challenges (and course corrections) in the future. The content of other challenges and conflicts may be different, but the human emotions and interpersonal dynamics needed to deal with them will be very much the same, as will be many of the street-smart moves needed to succeed.

A GIRAFFE STORY
continued

he has been instrumental in bringing diverse groups together—Israelis and Palestinians, Indian Hindus and Muslims—sometimes at his own peril. Living grant to grant has brought him financial dangers as well. But, Mednick says, "there are times in life when the service of man- and womankind has to transcend security. . . . Do the right thing. Life's short, and we all need to make the human choice in whatever we do."

Fred Mednick has made that choice, as has Jane Goodall, in her own work and in becoming honorary chair of her "little brother's" international advisory board.

Web link: Teachers Without Borders (www. teacherswithoutborders.org).

KEY POINT ■ *It's important that you and your group keep political interest and momentum behind the good solutions you've helped create.*

PLAY IT AGAIN

WHAT'S NEXT?
Creating change is a risky business. Have you got the nerve? The next chapter is about risk taking and courage.

■ *Your vision isn't worth much until you do* something *to make it real.*

■ *A good plan will keep you organized and focused, help you make the most of your time and energy, and definitely improve your odds of getting where you want to go.*

■ *Steps for visionary planning:*

■ *Review your problem, project, and vision, and the list of details you've created so far.*

■ *Expand and deepen the research you've already begun.*

■ *Identify the obstacles, risks, and resources that impact your project.*

■ *Brainstorm possible solutions.*

■ *Create an action plan.*

■ *Expect the unexpected.*

■ *Celebrate your successes.*

■ *Follow up and follow through.*

■ *Be mindful of your legacy. The strategies and tactics you and your team have developed, the tone and attitudes you've modeled, and the relationships you've formed can all be used to help tackle similar challenges in the future.*

CHAPTER SIX

It is very dangerous to try to leap a chasm in two bounds.
CHINESE PROVERB

━━━━━━━━━━━━━━ ■ ━━━━━━━━━━━━━━

RISK TAKING AND COURAGE

STICKING YOUR neck out as an active citizen is no video game—
if things get tough, you can't just press the reset button and start
over. Taking a risk for the common good always means daring to act
in the face of the unknown and always includes the possibility of
hurt or loss. Reactions from peers can be cruel, and conflicts with
people who like things the way they are can get nasty, especially if
those people are in positions of authority. The risks that come with
standing up for what you believe in are real. They can include

- *standing up for an unpopular idea when others are telling you to sit down and shut up, and when you could lose friends and the support of people important to you;*

- *speaking out in public, especially if you're not experienced;*

- *failing, especially in public, where you could be embarrassed or ridiculed, and where your reputation could suffer;*

- *going up against difficult and angry opponents;*

- *spending time and money you don't have;*

- *getting no response or a negative one when you reach out to someone;*

- *being the target of retribution for blowing the whistle on inept or illegal practices in business or government.*

AN OSTRICH NATION

The challenges faced by our communities, the nation, and the world are enormous. But have you noticed, when people are faced with a serious public challenge, how many of them still keep their heads in the sand, hoping that somebody else will fix what's wrong? Just when we need more Giraffes, we get more ostriches.

After more than two centuries of being free, this nation is far from brave. From the inner cities to the suburbs, too many citizens don't go to (let alone speak up at) public meetings, join community associations, hold their politicians to account, or set to work to solve public problems. Too few of us are willing to challenge authority— government authority, corporate authority—when that needs to be done. And the more numbingly commercial our culture becomes, the more people focus on stuff and pleasures they can buy rather than on contributions they can make. We're so risk averse, we're almost insulted when something unexpected happens that we don't like. "Life should be safe!" we demand, and to the extent that it isn't, we sue for pain and suffering.

If you think this is a rant, here's a comment I got from Toby Thaler, a well-respected Seattle lawyer and political activist: "It's my belief," Thaler writes, "that most people in most places over most of history just want to be left alone. They don't want to feel compelled by guilt or whatever to 'be involved.' They just want to be home, garden, cook dinner, have sex now and then, and not be bothered by the bigger world. Those of us who agitate and are active are about 5–10 percent as far as I can tell. And the greedy ones count on the other 90 percent staying that way. It's when the 90 percent starts getting its oxen gored—as in France in the late 1700s, or everywhere in the 1930s—that things start changing."

If Thaler is even half right, it's a major problem.

What's going on? Why this excess of caution? Why are so many people willing to just accept whatever's going on around them, even if they don't agree with it, even if they're whining and complaining about it?

My take on it is that some people have been taught to play it safe since childhood and they've never questioned that, so they've never gotten involved. For some there's been reasonable success on the career ladder, and life has become comfortable, even predictable. The prospect of risking any of that comfort is not appealing.

I also blame our media-soaked culture for helping create these unheroic times. News reports focus on sensational, negative stories—what went wrong and who screwed up today? The PR and advertising industries all too often focus on trivia and shallow stereotypes. Everything is driven by competition for ratings and sales. The overall message that's left under your skin after most evenings of commercial television is: "It's a scary, dirty world out there, beyond your power to change. Meanwhile, let us amuse you."

A society that feeds on such messages, millions of person-hours per day, becomes so determined to protect itself, so absorbed in its own amusement and so apathetic, that it leaves little ground for growing heroes. At just the time when we need more models of people sticking their necks out for what they believe in, our media gives us celebrities instead—people famous, not because they are heroes, but because of what they do in music or movies or sports. The commercial drumbeats turn us into a society of consumers marching toward the mall instead of citizens rallying to create great communities. And the sheer number of passive hours

A GIRAFFE STORY
JoAnn Burkholder

JoAnn Burkholder, a professor of botany at North Carolina State University, never dreamed that her scientific research could lead her into personal danger.

Burkholder heads a research group that made an unhappy discovery in 1989: an organism, *Pfiesteria piscicida*, was responsible for massive fish kills in North Carolina waters and was poisoning fish in waterways from Delaware to the Gulf Coast of Alabama.

Then the news got worse— Burkholder and her research team were getting sick, too. The symptoms were minor at first: shortness of breath, itchy eyes, headaches, and a slight forgetfulness. But, depending on their level of exposure to *Pfiesteria*, their symptoms intensified. Currently, 12 scientists from four different labs have serious, persistent health problems; Burkholder herself has had chronic bronchial infections and 16 bouts of pneumonia. Burkholder and her team have also documented these illnesses in people who fish these coastal waters. The scientists now conduct their research in a specially designed biohazard facility, using decontamination chambers, air locks, and hooded hazard suits.

Burkholder informed authorities in the eastern and southern United States about *Pfiesteria*, assuming that precautions before the tube trains us to live as spectators and not players.

TURNING IT AROUND—
THE GIRAFFE HEROES PROJECT

Since the early 1980s, the Giraffe Heroes Project has been going in the opposite direction, rallying people who care about the fate of our democracy and inspiring them to take risks for the common good (see the preface and also the Giraffe Heroes Project Web site, www.giraffe.org). We realized from the beginning that when challenges in our society go unanswered, it's almost never for lack of good ideas or good people. Rather, it's for lack of good people with good ideas who are willing to stick their necks out to put those ideas and ideals into action. The Project moves people to take such risks, not by preaching at them, but by telling them stories of other people already acting with courage and compassion. These "Giraffes" become models, inspiring others to get to work on problems important to *them* (see the dramatic stories of Giraffes JoAnn Burkholder and Casey Ruud, pages 78 and 82). By shining a bright light on the courage and compassion of ordinary people, the Giraffe Heroes Project presents a powerful alternative to the focus of mainstream media on the violent and the trite. Over the past 20 years, the Project has made a difference, but the opposing forces are strong, and the siren songs of our commercial culture can be overwhelming. Strengthening a civic consciousness in this country—making active citizenship

would be taken for eradicating this environmental and public health threat. Instead, governments and private industry turned on Burkholder.

Her reports showed that the worst *Pfiesteria* infestations are in waters full of wastes from pig and chicken farms and from phosphate mining. People in those industries did not want to hear this. Her own university disavowed her research; her professional reputation was smeared in the press; her life was threatened. She had to get an unlisted phone number and install a security system at her home. She was blackballed by several state agencies and had to hire an attorney to represent her against threatened litigation by the fishing and pork industries.

On the other hand, people working in the fisheries have urged her to keep speaking out, and she has received many awards for her contributions to environmental policy and education, including the Scientific Freedom and Responsibility Award from the American Association for the Advancement of Science.

Committed to science and to public health, JoAnn Burkholder continues to conduct her research, to teach, and to spread the word about this serious toxin, despite the opposition of vested interests.

the norm instead of the exception—takes contributions from many people, hopefully including you.

TURNING IT AROUND—WHY *YOU* SHOULD TAKE RISKS FOR THE COMMON GOOD

Sticking your neck out is, well, risky. You need to have good reasons for doing it. Here are mine.

■ If You Don't Act, the Problems That Concern You Will Get Worse

The limitations of government and business for solving the problems that affect our lives are enormous. There are no men or women on white horses to ride to the rescue. Our future is up to us—as individuals, as members of groups and associations, and as citizens.

Help our culture get its nerve back. Being an active citizen demands that you be willing to take the necessary risks for your ideas and ideals. Your country, your community, and the planet need your head, your heart, and your actions.

KEY POINT ■ *You can't insulate yourself from risks and still hope to solve significant problems in your community or the wider world.*

■ Take These Risks Because Doing So Will Make You More Successful

Of course risk takers can fail, and they can suffer loss and hurt. Years of Giraffe watching, and lessons from my own life, however, have convinced me that people who are willing to take risks to put their ideals into action are more likely to succeed—not just in their civic lives, but at home and at work as well.

Why? Because sticking your neck out for what you believe in focuses your attention, commitment, and energy. It puts you on top of your game. Taking risks for your ideals also earns respect and support from others; when they see you up there without a net, they're far more likely to take you and your message seriously and to become active themselves. Consider the example in the classic film *Twelve Angry Men*, in which one person's fearless pursuit of the truth turns 11 other jurors around.

■ Take These Risks Because Doing So Will Add Meaning and Passion to Your Life

I think that as a culture we are boring ourselves to death, willing to do the same thing without question, though with complaints. I see too many people operating under the delusion that they can lead totally safe lives, as if that were interesting, wise, or even possible. The delusion has given us too many Living Dead, people who've spent years doing mind- and spirit-numbing things because they've been afraid to risk the quest for lives with meaning.

Taking risks for your ideals feeds your spirit and helps you be fully alive. Whether or not you take them can be the most important choice you'll ever make.

■ Take These Risks Because Your Example Is Important

I travel a lot, and everywhere I go I find people hungering not just for solutions to problems, but also for examples of people who are making headway. That's why the Giraffe Heroes Project tells the stories of Giraffes—so that more people will have these examples of caring men and women sticking their necks out for the common good, and be inspired to take action themselves on issues important to *them*. The Project has just scratched the surface; this country and the world need hundreds of thousands of such heroes.

See yourself as such a model, not a superhero. Few of us will ever need to risk our lives, but all of us have opportunities to make a difference. Most of those opportunities won't grab headlines— they're often small challenges that don't ask huge responses from us, just responsible action by a caring citizen. By being that responsible citizen, by sticking your neck out for what you believe in, you're modeling the alternative to the passive griping that's infected the body politic.

■ Take These Risks to Avoid Regrets You Don't Want to Have

Ohio activist Evelyn Schaeffer makes this point perfectly: "How will I feel if I look back and know I could have tried to solve the problem but didn't?" she writes. "That's what propelled me into my first crusade, updating local zoning after I had lived here for 12 years. When people asked why I was setting myself up as a target for people like the man who said in a public meeting I ought to go back to Cleveland, I replied: 'In 20 years when everything I treasure about my community is paved over and franchised, I'm going to bitterly regret that I didn't at least try. If I fail, I fail, but I'll know that the result happened in spite of my very best effort.'"

■ Take These Risks Because There May Be Miracles There

Risk takers often find doors swinging open for them, almost miraculously. We've had that experience at the Giraffe Heroes Project. When we launch ourselves into doing what's got to be done—whether or not we've got the resources in place to do it—that's when the check arrives to fund the work, or the perfect volunteer walks in the door. When we're super-cautious, we seem to slog through the week, without any beautiful "accidents" to ease the way.

I'm not suggesting that you be rash or ignore the need for sound planning. I'm talking about those times when you *have* thought and planned as best you could, but moving forward still requires a leap of faith, a push into the unknown. In 2003, for example, when we decided to create a middle-school curriculum based on the stories of Giraffes, we didn't have a dime to do it. But all our experience told us that such a program was badly needed, and that teachers, donors, and foundations would see the value we saw. So we began creating *Voices of Hope*, a program that teaches kids how to read while it guides them into service projects in their commu-

A GIRAFFE STORY
Casey Ruud

"If you think you'll make a difference here, you're kidding yourself. Nobody makes a difference here." That warning came from a coworker who was welcoming Casey Ruud to his first day as a safety inspector at the Hanford Nuclear Reservation in Washington State.

Ruud took his assignment seriously, knowing that Hanford was using uranium and plutonium to make detonators for nuclear weapons. Accidents with these deadly materials could poison groundwater and farmland for centuries. Stolen uranium and plutonium could be used by this nation's enemies to make weapons. Safety was clearly a vitally important job at Hanford.

Hanford was built during World War II, so the buildings and equipment were aging. Ruud found dozens of cracks in equipment welds, every one of them dangerous. He found drums of plutonium, not secured safely in vaults as required by the plant's own safety rules, but just sitting in a hallway. Nearby, a child's toy wagon with coffee cans bolted to either end was full of nuclear detonators. He learned from a frantic worker that the plant had lost track of four 55-gallon drums of plutonium, and he uncovered falsified records about a shipment of plutonium that was supposed to be accounted for.

nities. Three grants arrived just in time to pay for the first print run. The work is funded and moving into kids' hands.

KEY POINT ■ *Reach for a life that feeds your spirit and is filled with meaning; stick your own neck out as an active citizen. Your commitment is vital to society's health—and to yours.*

TIPS FOR TAKING RISKS AS AN ACTIVE CITIZEN

There are smart ways and not-so-smart ways to take risks. Smart is better.

■ Lower the Risks by Getting Better Information about Them

You may find out that some perceived risks aren't risks at all, or are less significant than you first thought. People were afraid of eclipses when they thought eclipses were caused by an angry god. The risks disappeared when people learned that eclipses were predictable effects of the orbits of the moon, sun, and earth. You can improve your knowledge of the risks you see by questioning people more familiar with the situation than you are, and by doing research in books, newspapers, and magazines, and on the Internet.

WHAT'S YOUR EXPERIENCE? ■ *Have you ever been in a situation in which the risks you first perceived disappeared in the light of new information—for example, someone you thought was an opponent wasn't?*

A GIRAFFE STORY
continued

An engineer at the plant anonymously sent Ruud a book of flawed designs within the plant, confirming his suspicions that there were even more safety problems than he had found on his own. Ruud reported to his supervisors that Hanford was vulnerable to thefts by terrorists, to deadly fires, and to catastrophic explosions. Shutting down production to fix any of these dangerous conditions would be costly to the company, so the company did nothing.

But Ruud's criticisms were getting noticed even though nothing was changing. The company's contract to run the site, a job worth $4 billion, was at stake, and instead of fixing the safety violations, Hanford managers pressured Ruud to keep quiet. If he was "a good company man," he'd be well taken care of.

But Ruud was dedicated to safety, not to a company or to his own career advancement. The dangers remained, and Ruud took the next step. He blew the whistle by speaking to *The Seattle Times*, which ran a long and alarming story on the problems at Hanford. Ruud was called to testify before Congress, the Hanford plant was shut down, and a new company was brought in to manage the site.

Ruud had done the right thing, but he was a marked man. The new Hanford managers fired

On the other hand, if you increase your knowledge and find that the risks are real, the things you've learned can help you prepare to take those risks.

Many people tend to exaggerate the real risks they face, either because they haven't had much practice at taking risks or because they've got too many memories of risks that failed. It's also easy to load a real risk with lots of other emotional baggage that's just not relevant to the here and now. If you were cowed by your first-grade teacher or your drill sergeant 30 years ago, that experience could be adding to whatever uneasiness you may feel in speaking your mind to your boss, or to the mayor or the leader of the opposition.

TRY THIS ■ *Take the time to reflect on the nature of your fear. How much of it is fear of the specific risk in front of you and how much is baggage? Reflection may not eliminate the queasiness you feel, but naming the fear accurately will help you move forward.*

■ Lower the Risks by Increasing Your Competence to Take Them

Situations tend to be scarier the less competent we feel to handle them—often because we lack skills, plans, or support. Putting on a fund-raising event is more frightening if you have no idea how to do it. Overturning a county ordinance is more daunting if your team lacks a plan. Taking on city hall is scarier if you're all alone. You can use what's in this book to build your skills, make a plan, and enlist support.

him almost immediately. Some residents of his community feared that Ruud's disclosures would close Hanford forever, causing massive job losses. They ostracized him. Some parents told their kids not to associate with his kids. "Nobody would even sit next to us at basketball games," Ruud remembers. A pastor called Ruud "evil" and directed his congregation not to patronize the frozen yogurt shop that Ruud was running to support his family. The shop went out of business.

Ruud's dedication to public safety had enraged his employers, but it attracted the U.S. Environmental Protection Agency, which sent him back to Hanford as a *federal* safety inspector, one who could not be fired by the plant's managers. He went back to work, finding safety hazards and helping design a massive cleanup of the heavily toxic site.

He was still the most unpopular person in the community, and he still had to struggle against the managers' resistance to change, but the safety of people and the environment was at stake, now and thousands of years into the future.

"Sure it was hard," Ruud will tell you. "But it had to be done. When things got really tough, I did think of chickening out. But then I'd think, I'm a Giraffe. I've got to keep

Gaining experience is another important source of competence. You'll feel a lot more confident testifying before the planning commission if it's the fifth time rather than the first. You may want to begin with small challenges, with small risks, until you've built a track record.

Don't hold back now because you feel you're not perfectly competent or because you feel some butterflies. Take the first steps. Then up the ante, each time going one step past your present level of comfort.

A GIRAFFE STORY
continued

sticking my neck out. And I'd go on." (Ruud was honored as a Giraffe in 1990.)

Today Ruud is proud that attitudes toward whistle-blowers, worker safety, and the environment are improving, and that Hanford has changed. "The risk of a catastrophic accident at Hanford is minuscule now, compared to when I was there."

▪ The Secret to Being Brave

Getting better information and increasing your competence are pretty obvious ways to lower risks. I suggest them here because people so often rush into action unprepared. Slow down. Get better information and increase your competence by learning a skill, making a plan, getting support, and gaining more experience.

But information and competence can take you only so far. They can never reduce your perceived risks to zero. To face the risks that remain will take courage.

KEY POINT ▪ *Courage is not about being unafraid. Courage is doing the right thing, and doing it well, even when you are afraid.*

Where does courage come from? What makes one brave?

KEY POINT ▪ *You can increase your courage to face risks by focusing on the meaning that the risky action has for you.*

Chapter 1 discussed the importance of finding and leading a meaningful life, and of service as the path to meaning. Now I'm saying that there's an important link between meaning and courage. How does that work?

Think about it: when something you're doing is personally meaningful—a relationship, a job, a cause—you feel deeply that you're on the right path, you're committed to walking it, and you feel good about that.

If you have to do something that scares you in order to keep on that path, don't focus just on the risks. Look at them within the whole picture, as parts of this path you know are meaningful. When you see risks in this broader context, they don't go away, but they do seem more worth taking, and you become more willing, confident, and competent to face them. In other words, the commitment you already have for walking that meaningful path spills over onto the risks you face along the way, and you draw on the power of that meaning to help you act despite your fear. Here's a hypothetical example:

Let's say you've agreed to mentor a kid who is reading way below his grade level. But you quickly see that reading is the least of it. He's angry and he's starved for affection and respect, at school and at home. You see that you're not just helping with his homework—he's depending on you for much more. You feel like you're on a high wire without a net, with far more responsibility than you want. But if you chicken out, you could make things even worse for him.

You'll find the courage to deal with these risks by remembering what it means to you to be a mentor, helping shape a child's life for the better. Now you can see the risks in the context of doing something that's meaningful to you, so your inner talk can be, "I'm a mentor to someone who needs one badly, and doing this is really important to me. The risks that are scaring me now are a part of being that mentor—so here I go."

Many of the Giraffes whose stories are in this book are good examples of people who have become braver because they found meaning in the challenges that called them to be brave.

Something that happened during one of my bizarre adventures also illustrates the impact of meaning on courage. And it's a good example of the power of a role model:

CASE STUDY A Sinking Ship

Many years ago, I was on a ship in the Gulf of Alaska that caught fire in the middle of the night. As the fire spread, the abandon-ship signal was sounded, and 550 passengers and crew members were directed into lifeboats. The lifeboat procedures were chaotic; 95 people were wedged into our boat even though a big sign on the bow said that it was built for 48. We were 140 miles from the Alaskan coast. People were freezing cold, and a storm was building as we waited for dawn, the earliest that rescue helicopters could arrive.

There were a dozen members of the crew in that boat, including a couple of junior officers. They all looked very scared and none of them took charge. Then one of the seamen stood up in that jam-packed, pitching boat—a very bad idea—and screamed that we were all going to die. Several people started to wail.

An elegant woman in her 70s immediately stood up next to the ranting crewman, slapped him across the face, and told him to sit down. The man shut up and stared at her, stunned, while she lectured him on his bad behavior. He sat down, red faced. The weeping stopped. Somebody started leading songs. The moment of panic passed.

This magnificent woman was certainly aware of the extreme danger we were in. She may have been just as scared as the rest of us in that lifeboat, shivering and wet, watching the storm coming on. I think what separated her from the panicky crew was the meaning each put into that desperate situation—or didn't. Even with their training, the officers and crew in that lifeboat seemed to have no pride as men of the sea, and when they needed to be courageous, they weren't.

But that woman was from a family with a history of public service that went back to the American Revolution; acting for the common good *meant* something to her. You could see it on her face—quelling panic in a pitching lifeboat was the kind of service her family had always offered. Now it was her turn. Lives were at stake, so she stopped the panic, not only with her action, but also with her example. When that crewman lost it, some of the passengers started to follow his lead. But the woman led in the opposite direction, showing people that courage was in order, not panic. She reversed the mood and behavior of the group.

KEY POINT ■ *Committing to your ideals can put you in situations that scare you. But if you focus on the meaning that the action has for you, you'll take those risks, and you'll take them well.*

■ Keep On Keeping On

Of course, you can take risks and fail. You can be caring and responsible, your life and actions can all be meaningful, your plan can be terrific—and you can still fail.

It happens. You pick yourself up off the floor. You figure out how to do what you're doing better. And you start again.

KEY POINT ■ *It's not falling off the horse that's the problem—it's the lying there.*

There may be times when you look out at problems you might help solve and you just don't give a damn; your life at that point is not exactly brimming with compassion, courage, and meaning. And there may be times in the middle of a project when a string of setbacks has gotten you down and you want to quit. Keep reminding yourself at these difficult times of who you are in your best moments, and who you *can* be anytime you pull yourself together.

Finally, I understand how easy it is to be cynical about politics and government. I understand how easy it is to see other people behaving badly and to fill your life with blame instead of positive action. I understand how easy it is to see people making fortunes at others' expense and think that, yeah, you are entitled to your share, too—that society or life or "somebody" owes you comfort and ease.

Don't go there! That's the path of the Living Dead. Instead, remind yourself of how important it is for you to make a difference. Remind yourself that change happens only when people—not superheroes but ordinary people—see problems and do something about them, despite the risks.

If some idea or ideal for change is burning in you, the time comes in your life when you can't just talk about it anymore. You've got to stick your neck out and go for it. *That's* courage.

PLAY IT AGAIN

WHAT'S NEXT?

It's possible that not everyone will be enthusiastic about what you're doing. There could be trouble. Chapter 7 looks at finding common ground in negotiating and in resolving conflicts.

■ Taking a risk for the common good always means daring to act in the face of the unknown and always includes the possibility of hurt or loss.

■ When faced with a serious public challenge, too many people still keep their heads in the sand, hoping that "somebody" else will fix what's wrong.

■ Since the early 1980s, the Giraffe Heroes Project has been inspiring people to take risks for the common good.

■ Why should you take risks for the common good? Take them

  ▪ because if you don't act, the problems that concern you will get worse;

  ▪ because doing so will make you more successful;

  ▪ because doing so will add meaning and passion to your life;

  ▪ because your example is important;

  ▪ to avoid regrets you don't want to have;

  ▪ because there may be miracles there.

■ Tips for taking risks as an active citizen:

  ▪ Lower the risks by getting better information about them.

  ▪ Lower the risks by increasing your competence to take them.

  ▪ Gain courage to face risks by focusing on the meaning that the risky action has for you.

  ▪ Keep on keeping on.

■ If some idea or ideal for change is burning in you, the time comes when you've got to stick your neck out and go for it.

CHAPTER SEVEN

Never inflame the will of your opponent.
MAHATMA GANDHI

■

FINDING COMMON GROUND:
NEGOTIATING AND RESOLVING CONFLICTS

FINDING COMMON ground with other people does not mean finding absolute agreement. Common ground is shareable ground whose boundaries are marked by a range of actions that all can live with. You and your neighbor may not vote for the same political candidate, for example, but your shared belief in elections, free speech, and the democratic process is common ground.

Negotiating is a rational process for resolving differences and for finding common ground. It's not just what diplomats and labor and management leaders do—all of us do it all the time. We negotiate with our spouses over what color to paint the kitchen or where to go on vacation. We negotiate with the phone company over a bill we don't agree with. We negotiate with our employers to get a raise. We negotiate with our teenagers over curfews and car keys.

Active citizens negotiate within their own groups over strategies and priorities; with government officials over policies and funding;

and with other citizens, who may not understand or agree with what they want to do.

When negotiations are done well, they can bring people together instead of pushing them apart. They can lead to solutions that are smarter and fairer than either side may have originally proposed. They can even be fun.

But not always. When negotiations go badly (or are never attempted), the result is conflict; people become defensive, emotional, and, in the extreme case, violent in words and/or actions.

This chapter includes both general principles and tactical advice for negotiating good solutions, for keeping negotiations from becoming conflicts, and for resolving conflicts when they *do* occur. It deals with negotiation and conflict together because the two can quickly shift back and forth into each other, as reason and emotion jockey for control.

The suggestions here apply not just to negotiations and conflicts you may encounter as an active citizen, but also to those in any area of your life—at work or in your home, for example. People are people, and the interpersonal dynamics of dealing with differences are pretty much the same, regardless of the scale and complexity of the situation. If negotiating house rules with your teenager seems as hard as brokering peace in the Middle East, you may be right!

The strategy described below may be very different from other models you have used or read about. It doesn't depend on outwitting or overpowering an opponent, nor does it focus on bargaining over interests and positions. *It works by creating the trust needed to find and build on common ground.* Its goal is to find solutions that are stable because they bring people together instead of pushing them further apart.

I've used and refined this strategy over 30 years of negotiating and resolving conflicts, including face-offs at the United Nations and environmental battles in the Pacific Northwest. I've taught these principles for the last 15 years in hundreds of workshops and consultations. Of course, they don't always work. But a strategy based on building trust has dramatically raised the odds for my success, and I'm convinced that it will do the same for you.

Finally, negotiating is but one tool in a much larger tool kit for creating change. That kit, depending on the circumstances, might also include public testimony, bureaucratic maneuvering, mass-media initiatives, community forums, lobbying, electoral politics, litigation, and public actions such as boycotts and demonstrations. Many or even all of these elements can fit together as part of your overall plan for change (see chapter 5).

I've broken this chapter into two major sections. The first discusses general principles for negotiating and resolving conflicts; the second offers a 10-step strategy for actually doing it.

GENERAL PRINCIPLES FOR NEGOTIATING AND RESOLVING CONFLICTS

Some of these elements you already know; others may be new and challenging. All of them represent years of experience, on my part and others', of what works and what does not.

■ Winning at the Expense of Others Is a Poor Solution

Seeking unilateral victories often sacrifices long-term benefit for short-term "gain." People put on the defensive will usually fight back, which closes their minds to anything but "winning" (or surviving). Manipulating or overpowering people may get you to your immediate objective, but it's also certain to seed festering fears and resentments that will come back to hurt you or your cause; the enemies you make will wait until your back is turned, or until you've moved on, to counterattack.

WHAT'S YOUR EXPERIENCE? ■ *Have you ever been involved in a conflict that seemed to go on forever, with every minor "victory" by one side ratcheting up the conflict one more notch? If you have, what happened? How did it end? Did it end?*

Here's an example from my own past:

CASE STUDY
Island County

As leader of the Citizens' Growth Management Coalition, I had to keep a group of active and opinionated people working well together under conditions that were often stressful. Two years into the effort, the coalition had to make some difficult decisions about taking legal action to win changes where negotiations with the county had failed. For a time, our meetings became more stressful than usual—although that's no excuse for what happened.

One member of our group—call him Lloyd—never, in my opinion, quite seemed to understand what was going on. He did homework that I thought was shoddy. He muddied our negotiations with the county with irrelevant questions. He delayed coalition meetings with rambles that seemed pointless. At one particularly grueling meeting of our board, Lloyd was opposing almost everything I wanted to do.

I lost it. I cut him off and then proceeded to list all his failings in front of our entire group. I knew I had the votes to defeat him and I kept pummeling. Lloyd just sat there and took it, with a pained expression on his face. It was like hitting a chrysanthemum. Everybody else looked really embarrassed. I won all the points I wanted to win that night, but people couldn't wait to get out of that room.

Lloyd drifted off and ended up joining a group trying to block what the coalition was doing. A few people who were only so-so committed to the coalition became even less enthusiastic. And some of my friends and allies looked at me a bit suspiciously. I could almost hear them thinking, "Well, is *that* who John is? Can I *really* trust his judgment? And if he can be that nasty to Lloyd, maybe I'm next on his hit list!"

It took the coalition, and my leadership of it, months to recover from that mistake.

I had "won," but there are better options than creating winners and losers. It's possible to create real solutions to conflicts—solutions that will last because everyone is truly satisfied with them.

■ Look below the Waterline

Many negotiations and nearly all conflicts are like icebergs. Remember the discussion from chapter 2: the most dangerous part of an iceberg is not the part you can see, it's the part you can't. The top of the iceberg is the part of a negotiation or conflict that people talk about openly. But there's plenty below the waterline, too.

It could be a hidden agenda. A largely white community may try to block a low-income housing project by saying it will lower property values, but the real issue might be racism; they think all the new residents will be people of color, and they don't want those people in their neighborhood. Racism is one of the below-the-waterline issues that few people are willing to talk about.

Strong religious or political beliefs may be in full view, but often they are embedded in the iceberg, waiting for something to push them to the surface. Even deeper in the iceberg may be prejudices, fears, insecurities, or (especially) anger from past injuries and insults. Even if these buried elements have nothing directly to do with the problem at hand, they can significantly influence how people respond and how they behave. Habitual bullies, for example, may suffer from an underlying lack of self-confidence that's been feeding on them since they were kids.

CASE STUDY
The Peace Movement

When the Cold War was at its height and I was a "Cold Warrior" in the U.S. Foreign Service, I sometimes met with peace activists who wanted both sides to disarm their nuclear weapons. Their arguments made more and more sense, but I was amazed by how much personal hatred some of them had for the people making Cold War policy. That hatred was so intense that when people like me came to agree with them, these hard-liners couldn't accept that they had won us over. They were used to dealing with enemies, but they didn't know how to react when those enemies said, "You're right. I'm with you on this." When the Cold War ended, these people were at a loss—until they found new enemies to combat. For such people, the Cold War was the issue above the waterline of their iceberg. Below the waterline was a chunk of anger, perhaps put there when they were kids, that seemed to govern every move they made.

Sometimes you may be able to build enough trust with the other person to actually talk about buried issues, including your own. But no one's asking you to be a psychotherapist, and there's a limit to how deeply you can dig into somebody else's iceberg, let alone change what you may find there. Still, it's just common sense to recognize how buried issues and the emotions around them can make people defensive, unreasonable, and combative—and how those behaviors can undermine negotiations and make conflicts intractable.

For example, realizing that racist attitudes are behind a community's opposition to low-income housing won't end the racism, but it may help the advocates of that housing shape strategies that address those attitudes and even help soften them; the advocates could show community leaders successful low-income housing developments in other neighborhoods and urge them to talk with the residents. The goal would be to lessen stereotypes and provide examples showing that multiethnic neighborhoods can have a positive, respectful civic life.

Training yourself to look below the waterline will also help you be more sensitive and less judgmental with people in general. Don't excuse bad behavior—just acknowledge where it might be coming from and adjust your responses. If you suspect that Dan's bad temper is tied to his recent divorce, for example, then don't flaunt your own wedded bliss.

None of this is easy. After all, hidden agendas and other buried issues can be sensitive and even inflammatory—that's why they're hidden. Do this searching because at a minimum it will help you deal more constructively with emotions and attitudes around the table. And in the best instance, it can help you find solutions that are more likely to last because they take into account *all* of the elements in play. Ignoring major hidden elements—such as racism in a community—increases the danger that any "solution" you find will be at best a short-term fix, a compromise that breaks down with the first real challenge. The original problem will reappear, often in a different form.

▪ You're in Charge of Your Emotions, No Matter What the Provocation

An out-of-control reaction increases your provokers' control over you—and may cause a similar response in them, sending all of you over the edge.

I'm not suggesting you become emotionally dead. Showing your human side—joy, sadness, excitement—can be crucial to sustaining the personal intensity you need when things get tough. And by showing your humanity, you invite others to respond in kind, creating the connections that will help you both reach for common ground. My experience is that the air of "professional detachment" that many lawyers and consultants adopt often *prevents* this from happening.

It's letting fly with negative emotions, such as anger and frustration, that creates trouble. From my experience, when negotiations slide into conflicts and peo-

A GIRAFFE STORY
Azim Khamisa and Ples Felix

The bare facts of the story are these: Azim Khamisa's 20-year-old son, Tariq, was making a delivery for a San Diego pizza parlor when he was shot and killed in a robbery attempt by a gang. The killer was Ples Felix's 14-year-old grandson and ward, Tony Hicks, who was sentenced as an adult for the murder and is now imprisoned.

That could have been the end of the story. But it was only the beginning. Khamisa, a banker whose family had fled violence in East Africa years earlier, was devastated by his son's death, yet he reached out to the killer's family, realizing that they too had lost a boy.

Felix, a former Green Beret who is a program manager for San Diego County, was devastated by what his grandson had done—on the first night he had ever defied his grandfather and left the house to meet with the gang. Felix went alone to a gathering of the grieving Khamisa family, telling them of his own grief over what his grandson had done.

Khamisa established a foundation in his son's memory, and he and Felix formed an alliance that has transformed their losses into a resolve to see that other families do not suffer such tragedies.

"There were victims on both ends of the gun," says Khamisa. "Ples and I have become like brothers."

ple get stuck there, often it's not because they're too dumb to figure out solutions, but rather because they can't or won't deal with their anger and frustration well enough to work things out. That's true everywhere, from the Balkans to our own backyards. It certainly was true when my shouting at Lloyd hurt the Citizens' Coalition.

Anwar Sadat once said that the Middle East conflict was intractable, but not because of specific points of contention, such as West Bank settlements and Jerusalem. What made it so difficult, he said, was decades of rage. Your situation may not be the West Bank, but the point's still valid.

WHAT'S YOUR EXPERIENCE? ■ *Think of conflicts you've been in, at home, at school, at work—anywhere. Can you think of any that went on and on because people were stuck in anger and frustration they couldn't get past?*

Dealing with anger and frustration is almost always harder than dealing with the content of the conflict—especially if those emotions are tied to issues buried in the iceberg. Not taking the easy way can require a lot of self-control, but there's a lot to be said for being in charge of yourself instead of letting others jerk you around. And it doesn't take a lot of thought to see that lashing out will just make things worse.

What can you do the next time anger and frustration threaten to send a conflict you're involved in over the edge?

A GIRAFFE STORY
continued

Today Khamisa and Felix go again and again into schools—together—to talk to students about Tariq's death and about gangs, to help the kids talk about the awful effects of violence on their own lives, and to inspire the kids to affirm that they will avoid violence themselves. Kids hearing the two men's story and seeing them working together also get an unforgettable picture of a response to violence that is not more violence and hatred.

Commenting on their work in schools, Khamisa says, "Every time you talk one youngster out of committing homicide, you save two."

Both Felix and Khamisa are speaking out for *restorative justice*, a way of dealing with criminals that helps lawbreakers understand what they have done and make restitution to those they have harmed, rather than just sending them to prison. "The way we deal now with lawbreakers does nothing for those they have injured, for reforming the criminal, or for repairing society," says Ples Felix.

Web link: Tariq Khamisa Foundation (www.tkf.org).

Once you've managed that crucial bit of hesitation, do what you have to do to stay cool—count to 10, breathe deeply, fiddle with your keys, pray. . . . Take another look at the situation, this time trying to see it through the other's eyes; he or she is probably not all wrong. And in any case, it doesn't help to blame others for goading you into an angry response, no matter how bad their behavior might be.

▪ Building Trust Is Often the Key to Success

Chapter 3 talked about the role of trust and caring in creating change, and chapter 4 described how trust helps in building and sustaining teams. Now we look at the same principles used in still another way.

In negotiations, as trust develops, the talking becomes more open and cooperative. Trust reduces incentives to posture and play to the crowd, and it makes possible the kind of creative risk taking that leads people to generate or support bold new options for solutions. With trust developing, even difficult people begin to feel safe enough to be open in ways they wouldn't have risked before—which can often lead to dramatic breakthroughs.

I'm not talking about the kind of trust you'd need to tell someone your deepest secrets. I'm talking about the trust that says, "OK, we have different views. But I think you're being honest, that you'll keep your word, that you'd like to find a solution, and that you're arguing for what you really believe is the best course."

Trust-building becomes even more important in conflict situations because of its power to defuse anger, fear, and frustration. Trust can calm people down—including you—so that you can explore solutions that simply couldn't be seen before in the fog of emotions and ego that conflict can generate. Trust can embolden people to take a look at problems deep in the iceberg and to start dealing with what may *really* be driving the conflict. Once both sides begin to loosen their armor and climb down off their battlements, the discussions become less defensive and more honest. This is as true for global conflicts as it is for a fight with your spouse.

KEY POINT ▪ *If you're in a conflict, building trust may be the only thing that will allow you to find the common ground needed to resolve it.*

There are many ways to build trust, all discussed in more detail in chapter 3. Competence, accountability, and honesty build trust: everybody in the negotiation or conflict needs to know not only that you *can* do your job, but also that you *will* do it—and that you will tell the truth and keep your word.

Respect for others' experiences, situations, and viewpoints also builds trust.

But the critical factor, as we've seen before, is caring. Your success may depend on your ability to see the humanity that others share with you—to put yourself in their shoes as best you can and to actively listen to their concerns. Even one simple caring act—a kind word, a small favor—can open channels of communication and shift an atmosphere away from conflict and toward cooperation. Remember the story about how a gift of a map helped rally my neighbors to fill potholes on a shared road (see "A Caring Toolbox" in chapter 3).

Here's a weightier example:

CASE STUDY Communication Workers of Canada

Some years ago, I gave a series of workshops on conflict resolution for the leadership of the Communication Workers of Canada (CWC). For several years, the Canadian telecommunications industry had been in serious trouble, with many phone-manufacturing jobs moving to Mexico because of the North American Free Trade Agreement (NAFTA). Management (Northern Telecom) had already closed a few phone-manufacturing plants and wanted to close more. Jobs were evaporating. A strike seemed imminent—one that would be very costly to both sides and to the country.

We focused on the big picture in those workshops. NAFTA was creating a critical problem for *both* the union and management, and that fact made the traditional negotiating strategy of us-versus-them suicidal for both sides. Nobody could win if union and management simply scrapped over a smaller pie; the aim had to be to create a bigger pie. The union needed a negotiating strategy whose purpose was *not* to maximize union gains at the expense of management, but rather to build enough trust between the two so that both sides could agree on solutions to the NAFTA-created crisis coming down on both their heads. To get there, we had to bring the leadership of both sides to a better mutual appreciation of what it was like to be in the other's shoes.

In the union workshops we simulated a negotiation, with the union boss playing the role of the Northern Telecom CEO. Within 10 minutes a key truth emerged: *both union and management leaders were under very similar, intense emotional pressures*—on the one side from shareholders concerned about falling stock prices, and on the other from rank-and-file members concerned about job security. This discovery led to a rich dialogue between the "CEO" and the union leaders on the stressful predicament they both shared: trying to meet seemingly impossible constituent demands.

When the role playing ended, union officials saw the management position in a new and more sympathetic light. The union chief was convinced that if he could get his counterpart to see the commonalities he'd just seen, management would see the union in a new light, too.

That's in fact what happened when the real negotiations began a month later. Union leaders successfully coaxed their management counterparts to see how similar the pressures were on each side. Enough trust was established at a personal level to begin exploring entirely new options for solutions. Both sides looked for ways not to divide up the old pie but to create a bigger one.

Those talks led to decisions by management not to close a key plant in Ontario but instead to retool it to produce a higher-tech product line, and to retrain workers instead of laying them off. These innovative solutions (and the avoidance of a crippling strike) attracted government support, and the total package became a model for other Canadian industries forced to adjust to NAFTA.

Both the union and management made a courageous choice—one they had to struggle to defend to their own constituents. They could have dealt with conflict the way most industries do when labor and management can't agree: each side could have stayed focused on its own needs, dug in its heels, and seriously damaged their mutual long-range interests. In this instance, labor and management agreed on a different path. They put themselves in the other's shoes, they built some trust, and then they calmly and creatively focused all their talents on building new options that served all sides.

Building trust is best done face-to-face. Still, if geographic distance forces you to work by telephone, e-mail, and snail mail, you build trust the best you can. The principles involved are the same—they're just more difficult to put into use because it is so much harder to be personal from a distance.

WHAT'S YOUR EXPERIENCE? ■ *Think of a conflict in which you trusted a person on the other side, even though you disagreed with his or her views. Now think of another conflict in which there was no trust anywhere. How did trusting, or not trusting, affect your actions—and the result?*

Reality check: It's not always possible to build trust with people who don't agree with you. Despite your best efforts, some of them will try to take advantage of your attempts. You might collect a few bruises, and your memory of those bruises might make you reluctant to try trusting again.

My advice is to acknowledge these risks and take them anyway. Others usually *do* respond positively. And nobody—certainly not me, with all the scar tissue I've got—is suggesting that you be a pushover. If efforts at trust building fail, then you have to defend yourself. You put your armor back on, and at worst you've lost a few points early in the game.

■ Acknowledge Past Wrongs and Hurts

If the conflict has been around long enough to generate wrongs and hurts, it's important to acknowledge them, to apologize for any role in causing or supporting them, and even to make restitution if that's called for. Unless the wrongs and hurts are all from one side, this effort needs to be mutual. Don't hesitate to go first; your example may be the catalyst for others to act (see the extraordinary example of Giraffes Azim Khamisa and Ples Felix on page 96).

Acknowledgments and apologies help bring memories of past wrongs and hurts to the surface so that they can be dealt with openly—and forgiven if need be—instead of being left to sabotage negotiations from deep inside the iceberg. Acknowledgments, apologies, and forgiveness demonstrate honesty, convey respect, and open hearts, and because they do, they help build trust. Often they can lend new life to peacemaking efforts that have been stalled by mutual recriminations, whether voiced or silent.

<CASE STUDY> **The Middle East**

In the summer of 2003 I attended a weeklong gathering of Israelis and Palestinians on neutral ground in Switzerland, sponsored by an international conflict-resolution group called Initiatives of Change. The meeting started out angrily and continued that way until both sides agreed to simply let the people on the other side speak of the wrongs and hurts they felt, without interruption. This unburdening took three days. At the end of that process—and, I think, as a natural consequence of it—representatives from each side apologized for the suffering that had been visited on the other. Instantly a connection was made that had not existed before. It did not create peace in the Middle East; none of those people were senior leaders. But all of them had influence, and the understandings they gained were shared in their respective societies.

WHAT'S YOUR EXPERIENCE? ■ *Think of a negotiation or conflict you've been in—maybe in your own home—where one or both parties apologized for past wrongs or hurts. What impact did that apology have on finding a solution?*

TEN STEPS TO COMMON GROUND

The 10 steps below will help you deal with any negotiation or conflict. They're simple concepts that sometimes aren't so simple to implement.

▪ Understand the Perspectives of the People You're Dealing With

Simply understanding the issues on the table is not enough, although you must do that too.

Perspectives are the deep-seated influences and biases that color people's thinking and influence their arguments and actions. Perspectives are formed from many things, including politics, religion, race, and culture—some of it buried in the iceberg. Often perspectives are revealed by the vocabulary and definitions people use (the tax paid on the assets of a dead person, for example, is called an "estate tax" by those who favor it and a "death tax" by those who don't).

You'll never understand others' perspectives perfectly, but if you don't try, you risk becoming a prisoner of your own personal circumstances, operating on your own projections instead of what's really motivating other people. This can cause you to miscalculate and to miss opportunities for solutions that a more accurate understanding of the other person might uncover.

WHAT'S YOUR EXPERIENCE? ▪ *Have you ever tried to solve even a simple problem with someone who had a dramatically different political or religious perspective from your own? What happened?*

▪ Suspend Judgments

Unless and until they prove you wrong, don't look at people with whom you have differences as "opponents." That promotes a self-fulfilling prophecy. See them and treat them as fellow human beings who don't share your views. Give them the chance to treat you the same way. If they respond positively, your differences will be easier to resolve, sometimes *much* easier. If you're wrong, and they're determined to fight, then you have to defend yourself; you may have lost a little ground, but the chance for a breakthrough justifies the risk.

Moralizing is another great way to make sure the other person digs in. Once Nora starts with "I just can't believe how self-serving your position is," she's just made it much harder to solve the problem.

Be aware of any stereotypes you may have of the others, including of their appearances and mannerisms. You may have the experience that men with scraggly beards and tie-dyed shirts are all radicals, but don't assume that *this* man with a scraggly beard and tie-dyed shirt is.

You might not be able to eliminate your stereotypes overnight, but the more conscious you are of them, the better you can override them. As we all know, such judgments *really* annoy people—and hanging on to them tends to create self-fulfilling prophecies. If you start a negotiation convinced that the other person is always grouchy, she'll be more likely to give you exactly what you expect. By suspending your stereotypes, at least initially, you risk little while giving others the opportunity to respond positively—and to diminish any stereotypes they may have of *you* (see Giraffe Diane Bock's story on this page).

WHAT'S YOUR EXPERIENCE? ■
Think of stereotypes you have of people you've had conflicts with. Now think of stereotypes they might have of you. What effect have these judgments had on finding good solutions?

■ **Start Building Trust Early**

The more trust you can establish from the start, the more flexibility, patience, and self-control people will show if and when things get tough and emotions start clashing. Trust built early on is like money in the bank. Here are two strategies:

Find nonthreatening ways to start personal dialogues before negotiations even begin. Use social events connected

As Diane Bock watched the 1992 riots in South Central Los Angeles from her suburban San Diego home, she felt devastated, horrified, and helpless. "What," she asked herself over and over, "can one person possibly do about racial ignorance and hatred?" She dwelled on the question for months until she realized that "one person" was the answer: "These walls were put up one brick at a time, and they have to be taken down that way, too," says Bock. "One person at a time."

Seeing that people tend to stereotype races because they don't understand each other's worlds, she got to her next question: "If you have people whose universes never touch, how do you get them to connect?" Her answer was Community Cousins, a nonprofit organization she founded in 1995 to give families of different races opportunities to get to know each other. Its plan, which Bock based on her relationship with her own cousins, is simple: Two families of different ethnicities are matched as "cousins" on the basis of shared interests, locale, and ages of their children. Once matched, the cousins are encouraged to do things together, but nothing is forced. Friendships develop as the families get together on their own terms—to share children's outgrown clothes and toys; to attend picnics, baseball games, holiday gatherings, with the negotiation or even momentary asides. For local problems, you may well bump into negotiating "opponents" at PTA dinners, Little League practices, condo-association meetings, or other events where you share common interests. If no such ways present themselves, consider *creating* them: invite the others to a meal or a ball game, letting them know beforehand that you simply want to get to know them—and them to know you—better.

Use any of these opportunities to share personal stories and experiences that may have little or nothing to do with the problems on the table. The goals here are to get to know the others as human beings, to diminish stereotypes, and to begin creating some mutual respect that will be very important when real negotiating begins.

Focus on the most difficult people. You can often smooth the path of negotiations and defuse potential conflicts by focusing your efforts to build trust on the very people whom you sense might be hardest to deal with. You won't find an instant solution to your problem by doing this, and you won't change any lifelong attitudes or behaviors. But by going out of your way early to talk to difficult people, to listen to their concerns, and perhaps to take some simple caring action (such as getting a cup of coffee), you might make it more likely that they'll give you the benefit of the doubt later on. I understand that this may be hard, especially if there are grudges, but it costs you little, so why not try?

A GIRAFFE STORY
continued

or the Community Cousins family events that Bock hosts regularly.

Bock spends most of her time and a good deal of her own financial resources to keep Community Cousins going. She's been harassed and threatened for her efforts. But more disturbing to Bock—and more common—is people's lack of participation. Though many people agree that Cousins is a good idea, few of them actually make the effort to get involved. And getting involved is the point. It's "nothing heroic in terms of time or commitment," says Bock; it's just a matter of "small doses spread over time." But Community Cousins is growing, slowly and steadily.

It began with a pilot group of 39 families, and today there are 101 families participating in the Los Angeles area. Bock's next goal is to create a Community Cousins handbook, so that the idea can spread to other communities. Already two seedling efforts have been planted—one in Texas and another in Minnesota. Bock's dream is to provide, one by one, family by family, "the opportunity for one human to discover that another is not that different, that the 'they' is just 'us.'"

Web link: Community Cousins (www.cdincorp.com/cuzz/index.htm).

■ When Negotiations Begin, Outline the Differences Accurately, Calmly, and Consistently

Zero in on what's at issue. It's amazing how often people start to fight over stuff that's not really a problem. Don't presume what the mayor's attitude is on budget cuts, for example, until she's actually stated what she believes. Ask questions, listen to the responses, and give feedback until everybody's clear on exactly what the differences are.

CASE STUDY Island County

At one point in the Citizens' Growth Management Coalition's three-year negotiation with the county over land use, we were working with the county planning director to establish what kinds of nonresidential development would be allowed in rural areas of the county and under what conditions. The negotiations, which had been going very smoothly, suddenly screeched to a halt. A little prodding turned up an interesting fact: of the 106 land uses we were negotiating, only one—religious institutions—remained a problem; one of the commissioners, a man of strong religious views, feared that the new rules might not allow enough parking for Sunday services at churches. So we researched examples of how other rural counties handled parking for their religious institutions and came up with reasonable suggestions that met our needs and those of the commissioner. The negotiations went forward.

Frame the problems so as to reveal what's really at stake. It's the iceberg again—you don't want to struggle for a solution that turns out to be peripheral to the real dispute. If your school board is considering introducing a new health curriculum, haggling over its cost won't solve much if the real problem is that the program includes sex education and some members are opposed to giving such information to kids. Framing the issue to include attitudes on sex education will undoubtedly raise some hackles, but at least you'll be negotiating over what's really at issue.

Get more information if you need it. As the differences get clearer, you may see that some new and different kind of information might help bridge them. If so, take the time to get it.

Never move the goalposts. Nothing destroys trust faster than backtracking on something you've already offered.

After pinpointing the differences, prioritize them. This way, the negotiation can focus on the most important problems first.

■ Explain Your Position and the Rationale for It with More Candor Than You're Comfortable With

Be open with your "opponents," not just about the advantages of your position but also—within reason—about its uncertainties and downsides. Describe your feelings surrounding the problem. Don't be afraid to acknowledge gaps in your knowledge. Pretending to have capabilities and answers you don't is a dangerous tactic, if for no other reason than because it will undermine trust when you are found out.

After this honest explanation of your position, offer your analysis of the others' positions. Tell them what you'd do if you were in their shoes, and ask them to consider what they might do in yours.

It's amazing how often opponents will walk through this door if you open it and respond in kind, which can lead to real breakthroughs. Honesty is shocking. Openness can be contagious. Mutual vulnerability can increase each side's respect and trust for the other; people become less defensive and more likely to move discussions toward solutions.

Yes, but . . . if it becomes clear that your opponent will only take advantage of your openness, then put your guard back up; you'll have lost a little ground, but the gamble was still worth it.

At a tense point in the coalition's negotiations with Island County, when it looked as if everything was headed for a bitter court fight, I stood up in a public session and told the county commissioners what I thought would be the strong and weak points of the coalition's case. They stopped shuffling their papers and stared at me. Then I told them what I thought were the county's strong and weak points of law. I painted what by then was a fairly obvious picture of the pain and expense for both sides of a drawn-out court fight. And I asked for one more effort to tackle the problems out of court.

Of course it was a risk, although I thought a small one—the commissioners were smart enough to have guessed most of what I told them about the coalition's strategy. But the ball was now in their court. They had to decide, "What's Graham up to? What if he's sincere? And if the problems really are this obvious, maybe we *ought* to try again to solve them out of court."

On orders from the commissioners, the county's lawyer contacted me that afternoon, and we set up another round of out-of-court negotiations that this time succeeded in establishing significant common ground. I'd taken a modest risk by trusting that the commissioners wouldn't simply use what I'd said to hurt our case. They had taken one in return by trusting me. And both sides benefited: we reached agreement on some important issues without the delay and expense of having a judge decide them for us.

AVOID THIS MISTAKE ▪ *Don't be "open" as a manipulation. If the others find out they're being played by you (which they will), you'll be way worse off than you were before.*

▪ Continue Exploring for Common Ground

With the differences now clearly outlined, start listing all those things you have in common, starting with any goals you share.

Make a mental graphic of this process. See the common ground you find as the shared area of two or more intersecting circles (depending on how many parties are negotiating), with each circle representing the views and values of one of the parties.

Initially that common area may be very small. It may be nothing more at first than sharing a sense of frustration. In the Island County case, we started with something more than that: both the coalition and the county agreed on the need to protect the county's aquifer, to preserve the county's rural character—even if we disagreed on some of the means of doing that—and to avoid a long and expensive court fight.

Whether initially that common ground is a sliver or a big chunk, *the objective now is to step with the other people into that shared area and to work together to expand it.*

Expand common ground through dialogue, not debate. The goal of debate is to prove yourself right. The goal of dialogue is to discover and enlarge areas of shared agreement. Dialogue is more than just responding to another's point of view; at its best, it's putting yourself into another's situation and trying to look out from there. Dialogue creates the opportunity for negotiated solutions that last because they're built on the discovery of shared positions and values rather than on points scored.

Be as open and informal as you can, so that the others will be encouraged to respond in kind. Finding commonalities can relax people, diminish stereotypes, and make communications easier; people become more open and less defensive in ways they might not have risked before.

Even small things that may be totally unconnected to the negotiations count. You might find that you went to the same school as someone across the table, for example, or that you both have kids in day care or share a love of golf. It all helps expand the shared area of those intersecting circles.

Build the momentum. Small commonalities lead to larger ones. As new common ground appears, keep adding details that expand it further. Nudge the conversation toward more and more sensitive issues, looking for more agreement. This takes an investment of time, so be patient. It's not necessary—or realistic—that the circles of interests will ever overlap completely.

I was once on a three-person county panel to make recommendations on wetlands protection. I represented the environmental community. The other panel members were the county planning director and a big-time land-use consultant, representing developers. All three of us had tangled before, and we rarely had agreed on anything.

The only common ground we really had was sports, so, especially in the beginning of a process that went on for six weeks, we talked a lot about sports, from the local soccer leagues to the Seattle Mariners. Those conversations relaxed us, established a common interest, confounded some ugly stereotypes we had of each other, and let us see each other in a context outside the conflict. We started listening more respectfully to each other's ideas, not just on the Mariners' bullpen, but also on wetlands. With our dukes down, we began acknowledging good points in each other's positions and looking for solutions we could all accept. We came to an agreement on wetlands that satisfied all sides. That wouldn't have happened if we'd slugged it out.

An important piece of the common ground forged between the consultant and me in these exchanges was the realization that if the two of us agreed, the county would bend over backward to implement our agreement, so eager was it to see the matter settled. In other words, *the very fact that developers and enviros were in agreement provided us leverage over county land-use policy that neither of us would have otherwise had.*

- ## Create New Options

With some common ground now clear to everyone and with some trust established, you can leap ahead: challenge all sides to look at the conflict with fresh eyes and to generate new options for solutions that are not just clever ways to divide up the old pie but ways to make a bigger pie.

When this process is really working, people begin to see the problem itself as the opponent. The situation is no longer "me against you" but "all of us against the problem we need to solve." People begin to use their energy and imagination not to play defense but to find solutions that didn't seem possible or couldn't be seen before—and to accept good ideas and insights no matter who suggests them. Dealing with conflict then becomes a deeply fulfilling experience—a demonstration that trust, courage, honesty, and common sense can triumph over fear and divisiveness.

When a promising new option emerges, keep talking about it, adding details and examining objections. Sometimes the most crucial move in this process is to look for and suggest face-saving outs that could make it easier for people to climb down off positions that had been strongly held and to accept new ideas.

CASE STUDY Island County

In the coalition's push for stronger protections for wetlands and streams in Island County, farmers were among our fiercest opponents at first. Their perception was that new environmental rules would threaten their livelihoods. It was a classic us-against-them situation.

When we started in 1997, it was very hard for the farmers and the coalition to even talk to each other, let alone negotiate solutions to sensitive issues. Both sides had their stereotypes: to many on our side, farmers had no concern for the environment; to many farmers, environmentalists were all selfish and elitist. The common ground we shared seemed a tiny sliver indeed.

We knew we had to build some trust between our groups before we could even hope to deal with the policy concerns. Otherwise we'd end up in court, which nobody wanted. So we started meeting, led by people on each side who were willing to take the risk.

Our initial meetings were awkward, but slowly we began to get the feel of what made each other tick and to put ourselves in each other's shoes. We quickly discovered that both sides had a genuine love for the land, and it didn't take much talking to also agree that preserving working farms was a key part of preserving the county's rural character. The enviros began to appreciate the farmers' shaky financial situation and to respect the responsibility most of them felt to be good stewards of the land. The farmers began to learn that the enviros weren't arrogant elitists but neighbors concerned about protecting habitat and water for everybody.

The more we began to appreciate the others' situations, the more we began to trust the others as intelligent and fair-minded people with different views on many issues. That sliver of common ground began to grow.

When we did start talking about the hard issues that divided us, the atmosphere was calmer, less defensive, more respectful—and more trusting—than it had been. We eventually all got so committed to solving the problem that in the end it was an enviro who suggested a part of the solution that the farmers might have come up with, and a farmer who proposed what the enviros might have proposed. We worked out a deal that both sides could live with—and *are* living with—for the long term.

Sometimes it helps to bridge an impasse if the two principals in a negotiation meet one-on-one, without others present. Even if you don't find a solution, such meetings can help avoid public fights that will only entrench the positions of both sides. When it got down to the nitty-gritty in some of the coalition's negotiations with Island County, for example, what broke through was a quiet talk between the county's lawyer and me.

AVOID THIS MISTAKE ▪ *The caution here is that if you are the principal and you do engage in side conversations, you must make sure to inform the others on your team of what you are doing and why, in order to avoid misunderstandings.*

▪ Approach Trade-offs with Care

Especially in a long and tiring negotiation, it can be very tempting to start focusing on trade-offs— "You give us A if we give you B."

The biggest danger of focusing on trade-offs is that this strategy easily can degenerate to "splitting the difference," which doesn't often produce good long-term results. Yes, it does allow both sides to declare victory and save face, at least initially. But my experience is that it's often just an excuse for ducking the tough issues instead of resolving them, usually because one or both parties are so tired that they just want the fight to go away. Splitting the difference can cause you to lose sight of your negotiating goals—peace at any price becomes the goal. And it often just postpones issues instead of resolving them.

WHAT'S YOUR EXPERIENCE? ■ *Have you ever been in a conflict in which, tired of fighting, you agreed to split the difference with the other person? What was the result? Was the conflict really solved?*

If a tempting offer is made to your team in a negotiation to split the difference, step back and look at the total issue again. Go back to the team's vision of success. Would accepting this offer get you to your vision or even close—or would it be a cop-out?

KEY POINT ■ *Trade-offs in a negotiation work best when they leave all sides better off without burying important issues or sacrificing a principle important to anyone.*

To find "good" trade-offs, look for what professional negotiators call *offsetting asymmetries*. An asymmetry is when each side puts a significantly different value on the same element. Offsetting asymmetries are when there are two (or more) of those asymmetries in play, with each side having at least one element valued higher by the other side than by itself. For example: Let's say you and I are trading baseball cards. I have an extra Alex Rodriguez. You, on the other hand, have been trying to get your hands on an Alex Rodriguez for months. You've got an extra Roger Clemens, which I'd dearly like to have. If we trade an Alex for a Roger, we both win. Both sides see the trade not as a gain and a loss but as part of a common-ground solution they have contributed to that benefits all sides.

Here's a real example of how offsetting asymmetries can work:

CASE STUDY Island County

As noted above, as part of its long struggle for good growth management in Island County, the coalition negotiated directly with farmers over zoning and regulations for agriculture. For the farmers, the key issue was financial flexibility—they very much wanted the right to develop a portion of their land. Most of them wanted to stay on the land—they just wanted some of it to be zoned for development so that they could use it as collateral for bank loans or to send a kid to college.

The coalition was willing to agree to some financial flexibility (we saw it as an incentive to help farmers stay on the land), but what we really wanted were tougher new rules for protecting groundwater by fencing off streams and wetlands from livestock. The farmers could live with tougher rules for fencing. Until these negotiations, their resistance was fueled less by the new rules than by their perception that they alone were being asked to bear the financial burden of providing the county's rural character. Our negotiation at least lessened this perception.

The result was a very creative agreement that let each farmer develop 15 percent of his land (under carefully prescribed conditions) in return for agreeing to implement tougher new rules for grazing and fencing. Both sides ended up ahead.

■ Build an Agreement on the Common Ground You Find, and Commit to Carrying It Out

If you've found a solution that all sides can accept, don't stop now; you're almost to the goal line. Nail down the details of your agreement in writing, and develop a plan and timetable for carrying it out.

The devil is in the details. If you discover that some details for implementing an agreement are still disputed, go back to the common ground you built inside the overlapping circles and work your way forward again until the details are clear. What was the picture both sides saw inside that common ground? What were the principles they agreed on? In the Island County case described just above, the original agreement did not specify with enough precision just where, on a farmer's total acreage, the 15 percent of developable land could be. Revisiting the negotiation, it was clear that both sides saw the house sites on high ground—not on lowlands suitable for crops—and words were added to the county code to reflect that.

■ Celebrate Success

Take every opportunity to express to the other side your appreciation of agreements made with them and to celebrate your negotiating successes together. It's positive reinforcement—and it also encourages others to follow your lead in the conflicts *they* face.

IT DOESN'T WORK EVERY TIME

Sometimes the issues on the table truly are intractable. Sometimes the people you're dealing with really are unmovable. Sometimes the issues below the waterline of someone's iceberg are simply too deep and too powerful. If that's the case, you can still drop back and try to use more conventional tactics to hammer out a compromise. Or you can let the courts decide, which introduces a whole new set of risks (see "Legal Action" in chapter 11).

KEY POINT ■ *What's important in setting your negotiating strategy is to assess each situation on its own—and to be very honest about the risks. If you feel yourself backing away from being more open, caring, and trusting than you're comfortable with, ask yourself whether you're making a true appraisal of the odds, or rationalizing so that you won't have to risk making the first move in those directions. Pulling back from the attempt to build trust with an "opponent," before it's clear that you must, may eliminate opportunities for real breakthroughs.*

It *does* take more courage to use the strategy outlined above than to square off and fight. Fighting is what we know how to do; it's what everybody expects. Dividing ourselves up into good guys and bad guys means that we can con ourselves into thinking the issues are simple when they're not. All the options for doing something better are invitations to step into uncharted territory, where there are no quick stereotypes and easy answers, where the search is for options that cut through fear instead of increasing it, and where the tools are not easy ones like anger and manipulation, but tough ones like caring, responsibility, and moral choice.

It's not an easy decision—at least it wasn't for me. I was slow to realize that most of the conflicts I was engaged in were preventable and unnecessary. I finally saw that humans would never end conflicts, personal or global, until we were willing to take the risks to try something new—to be more open and vulnerable, to care, to build trust. As I began to see how powerful these elements were in negotiating differences and settling conflicts, I got braver about using them, and I began to build a positive track record. Twenty-five years later I can say that building trust has consistently brought me better results in negotiating and in dealing with conflict than trying to "win" at another's expense.

KEY POINT ■ *Building trust breaks the rules of the tired old game of blame and counter-blame, and it reverses the negative momentum of conflicts that have begun to move in vicious circles.*

To me now, it makes no sense not to try.

PLAY IT AGAIN

WHAT'S NEXT?
Persuasive communications are a vital element of effective citizen action. The next chapter covers speeches, fund-raising, and more.

■ *Finding common ground does not mean finding absolute agreement. Common ground is shareable ground, whose boundaries are marked by a range of actions all can live with.*

■ *Negotiating is but one tool in a much larger tool kit for creating change.*

■ *General principles:*

   ■ *Winning at the expense of others is a poor solution.*

   ■ *Look below the waterline. There you may find hidden agendas, strong religious or political beliefs, and prejudices, fears, and insecurities or (especially) anger from past hurts and slights.*

   ■ *You're in charge of your emotions, no matter what the provocation.*

   ■ *Building trust is often the key to success. The key to building trust is caring.*

   ■ *Apologize for past wrongs and hurts.*

■ *Ten steps to common ground:*

   ■ *Understand the perspectives of the people you're dealing with.*

   ■ *Suspend judgments.*

   ■ *Start building trust early.*

   ■ *When negotiations begin, outline the differences accurately, calmly, and consistently.*

   ■ *Explain your position and the rationale for it with more candor than you're comfortable with.*

- Continue exploring for common ground. See the common ground you find as the shared area of intersecting circles.

- Create new options.

- Approach trade-offs with care.

- Build an agreement on the common ground you find, and commit to carrying it out.

- Celebrate success.

- This strategy doesn't work every time, but using it will definitely raise the odds of your success.

*It is becoming evident . . . that a single, seemingly powerless
person who dares to cry out the word of truth and to stand
behind it with all his person and all his life, ready to pay a
high price, has, surprisingly, greater power . . . than do
thousands of anonymous voters.*

VACLAV HAVEL,
"Politics and Conscience"

■

PERSUASIVE COMMUNICATIONS: SPEECHES, FUND-RAISING, AND MORE

LEARNING HOW to communicate may start when we're infants, but mastering the skill is a lifelong challenge. This chapter will help you whether you're trying to sway a hotel ballroom full of people or just get a point across to your team. Chapter 9 covers media and public relations, and chapter 10 includes participating at public hearings and lobbying.

PERSUASIVE COMMUNICATIONS—STYLE, ATTITUDE, HEART, AND VISION

As we all know, it's important to engage your brain before your mouth. Rash statements, rash e-mails, and rash letters all create holes you just have to spend time and effort digging out of—if you can. Keeping your cool is often not easy, especially if you're being attacked (see the story of Giraffe Claudia Johnson on page 124). But there's a lot more to successful communications than staying calm.

■ Know How You Come Across to Others— and Adjust if You Have To

KEY POINT ■ *Good communicators are conscious of how others might perceive them and can adjust their style to make better connections.*

For example, I'm a 200-pound, six-foot-four, deep-voiced male who's used to giving speeches in hotel ballrooms. My problem is not in being noticed but in coming across so strongly that I put some people on the defensive. Talking to a small group in somebody's living room, I often need to remind myself that I'll connect to people better if I throttle down my voice and avoid big gestures. Often I'll find a way to sit down so that I don't tower over shorter people. Clothes are part of communication, too, and in my case I found that people became more comfortable around me (and more receptive to what I was saying) when I gave up dark blue power suits and red ties. Sport coats and slacks are more comfortable for everybody—including me.

Once, during a seminar in negotiating techniques, I asked a trade union's leaders to do mock presentations to each other. One of the participants was a large, motherly, very dominant Irishwoman named Mary. I noticed immediately that many of the younger men "negotiating" with Mary in these practice sessions became defensive. I was even feeling it myself. What was going on? Finally it hit me: Mary could be making a sophisticated argument about wages and benefits, but she tended to look grim, to wag her finger, and to look exasperated and angry. What her young male adversaries heard was their own mothers saying, "Eat your peas or no dessert." Once Mary realized this (and could laugh about it), she softened her gestures and tone of voice and did much better.

■ Stay as Personal and Informal as You Can

The more important a communication is, the more people worry about making a mistake; the more they worry, the more formal and stiff they become, which—unless you're giving a deposition at an inquest—is almost always a mistake.

Yes, the prospect of an encounter with a political opponent, a major funder, or a VIP might make you nervous. Acknowledge the jitters if you feel them, but also acknowledge that you got this far by using what's in your head and heart *and it's all still there*. So lighten up and be yourself. Use the vocabulary and mannerisms you normally use and are comfortable with.

TRY THIS ■ *Imagine yourself just talking to a friend or group of friends, sitting in overstuffed chairs in a comfortable living room.*

Speaking isn't the only form of communication that benefits from a more personal and informal style. A handwritten note, or a printed letter with a handwritten note on it, will get people's attention faster than something that's been entirely word-processed. A face-to-face meeting is better than a telephone conversation, and a live phone conversation is better than dueling answering machines.

E-mails can get *too* informal. It's easy to forget that e-mails can be dispersed around the planet in an afternoon and preserved for a long time. I assume that every e-mail I write might get to hands I don't intend, and I'm especially careful with my tone and use of words.

■ Communicate a Vision

If you're trying to persuade a listener to change an attitude or take on a task, you'll do much better if—in addition to describing the problem—you communicate a compelling, hopeful, achievable *vision* of future possibilities.

You should be an old hand at visions by now. Chapter 2 described visions as clear, concrete pictures of how things could be. Communicating a vision requires no magic. It's about calling up your deepest, most powerful picture of the situation you'd like to see, and then painting that picture with as much clarity as you can. Visions breathe life into facts, they convey passion, and they inspire people to action.

Chapter 2 also showed you how to create a vision (you might want to review that part now). Chapter 4 discussed the value of a vision to a team and chapter 5 was about visionary planning. You can apply the same concept to communications—from personal letters to speeches to brochures to billboards. All of them will be more persuasive if you include a vision of the end results you want people to see, and then challenge them to step into that picture with you and help make it real.

■ Listen

Communicating is a two-way process. The more sensitive you are to the person you're talking to, the more effectively you'll shape and deliver your message. Actively invite feedback and acknowledge it. And do more than just listen to the other's words—watch body language and, as best you can, sense the feelings behind the words and gestures.

■ Be Conscious of the Little Things

How you answer the phone, meet people, wait in line, introduce newcomers, buy a newspaper, or even answer a roll call can affect the mood of everyone who sees or hears you, and therefore influence their reaction to your message. If in these little things you're distracted, unfriendly, sarcastic, or critical, it can push other people's moods in that direction—with consequences you'll never know. If, on the other hand, you handle these little things with caring, respect, and humor, you're helping create a more positive atmosphere. The same thing applies to nonverbal communications like wording a note or answering an e-mail.

TRY THIS ■ *Think of some routine interaction you have with another person. Maybe it's the waitress who brings you your coffee in the morning or the handyman in your apartment building. Consciously make your communications with that person warmer and more positive than usual. Maybe nothing happens the first few times you do this, but look again after you've kept it up awhile.*

These examples are easy. But now fine-tune the advice. Does anyone in your group have sensitivities that might need special handling—for example, political or religious beliefs that might be offended? Are you talking to someone who's learning English and might not get your jokes? Who needs directions repeated three times? Who tends to charge off before hearing them even once? The better you get to know people as individuals and the more you can put yourself in their shoes, the better you'll communicate with each one.

Taking the time and making the effort to tailor your communications to specific individuals is about more than just getting the message through. It's about your taking full responsibility for your impact on other human beings, who may be looking to you for information, guidance, inspiration, or reassurance.

■ Don't Send Mixed Messages

Watch for inconsistencies between the content of your words and your body language and tone of voice.

Body language often contributes to mixed messages, if only because it's so often unconscious. Think of people you've heard make optimistic statements about, say, health, money, a relationship, or any other goal when their face muscles were sagging in despair and their voices tired and faint: "We're sure that grandfather will be well soon." "We're confident that fourth-quarter earnings will be better." "I know she/he will come back to me."

Anger is another message that people often think they're hiding but aren't. Phil arrives at the meeting still steaming from a fight he's just had with his wife. You know him well, so you say, "Phil, you seem upset—want to talk about it?" Phil says, "No, no, I'm OK," when the veins on his neck are bulging, his color is that of a tomato, and every other aspect of his being suggests that he's ready to put his fist through a wall.

Those dark blue power suits I got rid of are another case in point. I was trying to show audiences how to solve conflicts by seeking common ground, but my clothes implied that I wanted to conquer my opponents.

Who said that English isn't a tonal language? Take the one-word response, "Great." Depending on the tone of voice, that word can mean anything from honest and enthusiastic approval to sarcastic dismissal. Be conscious of the tones you use.

HOW TO GIVE A GREAT SPEECH

I know people who'd rather go over Niagara Falls in a barrel than give a speech. But there are definitely times when being an active citizen means teaching courses, chairing meetings, testifying before public bodies, making presentations to schools and civic clubs, and more. The longer you stay involved as an agent for change, the more likely it is that you'll be called on to make public presentations of some kind.

▪ What, Me Worry?

One reason why many beginners are frightened of speaking in public is that they think public speaking invites being judged as a person. What will people think of *you*—of your appearance, your intelligence, your motives, your words?

Public speaking becomes less frightening as you gain experience. If you want to build your skills as a speaker, practice. Start with presentations to small audiences of people you know and like, and who will give you honest and constructive feedback. Watch experienced speakers and notice what they do. If you have access to video equipment, tape yourself practicing and doing presentations. Learn from what you see. And keep in mind that learning to speak in public is a valuable life skill; the risks and effort necessary to become a good speaker are worth it.

Learning how to speak well doesn't mean your goal has to be about bringing a thousand people to their feet, cheering. Just getting your points across in a coherent fashion can be a triumph if you thought you could never do that.

But you *can* do that. Whether you are a beginner or have experience, the following points will help you.

■ Before You Start

Fulfill the bill. Be absolutely sure that you and the event's sponsors are on the same page regarding the theme of your speech. Lapses here can be embarrassing. I once gave a marvelous speech on volunteering to a thousand people assembled by a large social-services agency. The only problem was that the agency had expected me to give a fund-raising speech—they already had plenty of volunteers. I fault them for not clearly communicating their intentions, and I fault myself for not paying enough attention to avoid this avoidable mistake.

Know your subject—and your audience. Especially if your subject is complicated, go over the details enough to be sure you've got them right. If someone who wasn't there to hear you dissects the transcript of your speech, would he or she spot bad data, unsubstantiated claims, or lapses in logic?

It's also important to learn as much as you can in advance about the people you'll be talking to, so that you can start from where *they* are. What's on the minds and in the hearts of the people who will hear you? Audiences will respect and appreciate this extra concern on your part; they'll pay closer attention to what you say and be more willing to give you the benefit of any doubts.

Before you speak, question people familiar with this audience. Make a few phone calls to people who will be in the audience. You can also learn a lot by finding out who's spoken to this audience in the past and how people reacted to those speeches. I find that people are almost always willing to help guide me in this way, because they know they're helping make my speech more relevant and interesting.

Here are the things you most want to know about your audience members:

- *What competence in this subject do they already have? You don't want to tell them a lot they already know—but you also don't want to assume that they know more than they do.*

- *Are there any land mines you might step on—sensitive attitudes, beliefs, or history that might prompt negative reactions you haven't anticipated? I'm not saying that you shouldn't address the land mines if you want to—just know where they are.*

- *What special concerns might this audience have that would help connect it to your message? If you find out that your audience will consist mostly of young parents, for example, then you might want to stress the relevance of your subject to raising children.*

A GIRAFFE STORY
Claudia Johnson

Writer-professor-activist Claudia Johnson is sure that reading *Lysistrata* and *The Miller's Tale* when she was a student changed her life; those two classic works made her think and made her laugh—two things she's been doing ever since.

Her book *Stifled Laughter* tells the sometimes frightening story of her battle to save those very works from being banned from the public high school in Lake City, Florida. When some local parents demanded that the works be banned because they were "pornographic," were "blasphemous," and "promoted women's lib," Johnson was so concerned that she stuck her neck out to challenge the banning, first in the community and then in a long, expensive, and grueling journey through the courts.

Johnson was attacked in the newspaper, at public meetings, and in threatening phone calls. She kept to the high ground, explaining the principles of separation of church and state and freedom of expression, talking about students' right to read and learn from the classics so that they understood cultural history and could analyze challenging ideas.

The uproar was agonizing for Johnson and her family. While the case was in the federal courts, they moved to Live Oak, Florida. But instead of

If your audience is made up of members of one organization, have there been any significant recent events in that organization you should know about—so that you can either relate them to your subject or avoid them? If you're speaking to a Rotary Club that's just received a special service award from the governor, be sure to congratulate the members. If you know that the CEO of the company you're talking to has just been fired, you may not want to mention his name.

Make an outline of what you want to say. An outline will help you organize your presentation with a logical flow from beginning to end. If, for example, you're giving a speech to persuade people to join a community initiative, your outline might contain these points, more or less in this order:

- Introduce yourself.

- Describe the challenge you will talk about.

- Tell your audience members why they should care about this challenge, too.

- Give your audience a compelling, hopeful, achievable vision of what the future could be with that challenge met.

- Suggest a plan for action and show how it can be achieved.

- Invite the audience members to join you; tell them what they can do and explain how that will help.

- Briefly recap your main points.

- End with an inspiring story and a further call to action.

A GIRAFFE STORY
continued

finding respite there, Johnson was appalled to discover that parents were trying to ban *Of Mice and Men* from their high school. She and her husband also found their almost-finished house burned to ashes in a suspicious fire.

Johnson and her family rebuilt the house, and, despite renewed attacks on her personal integrity, she used everything she'd learned in Lake City to stop bannings in Live Oak.

She has continued to work tirelessly against censorship—speaking, writing, educating, inspiring, organizing, and helping others create grassroots anti-censorship coalitions in their own communities.

"Communities across America are being ripped apart by this issue," she reports. Johnson knows where she stands. "People who ban books believe children are fundamentally weak," she says. Claudia Johnson believes kids are smarter and stronger than that. She knows that a full and broad education makes them even stronger.

Reflect on the importance of what you're about to do. The first purpose of any public presentation is to forge trusting connections with the audience and then to use those connections to help make the world—or your part of it—better. I think this is true whether you're struggling to get your town council to approve bike lanes or sharing your ideas on the Middle East. I think it's true whether you're talking to a huge hall full of people or the early morning crowd at Kiwanis. See yourself as an agent for doing good.

Personalize that effect. For some, your presentation will be the only opportunity they'll have to learn about your issue. For some, your presentation may so excite them that they'll pursue the issue on their own. Finally, the positive example you put forth—your courage, compassion, thoughtfulness, and commitment—may inspire people to do better on some issue that has nothing to do with the subject of your speech. I know from experience that any or all of these things can happen, and often do.

Anticipate good results. Just before you go on, close your eyes and picture the audience reaction you want. See the animated faces of people waiting for your next words. Feel the connections you are forging. Sense the flow of energy back and forth between you and the audience. Listen to the laughter and the applause.

■ When the Presentation Starts

Take control of the introduction. Usually somebody else will introduce you. That introduction is important because it can help set the tone for your speech. If your introducer drones on with a laundry list of your achievements, it suggests to the audience that it's in for a long evening.

Don't assume that your introducer will get it right. Give him or her a few paragraphs to draw on, focused on a few key professional and personal items that will help your audience look forward to what it's about to hear. Suggest that your introducer focus on whatever personal experience he or she may have of you.

Emphasize that shorter is better. The introduction of you *should* be incomplete, because your personal story is a key part of your presentation—and nobody can tell that as well as you can, using anecdotes that support points throughout your speech.

Don't let your introducer steal your best punch lines. I often end my speeches with a story of some personal adventure, for example, but if the introducer has already mentioned that adventure, then some of the suspense is lost.

If the presentation is participatory, as in a workshop, ask people to introduce themselves as well, giving not just their names but also their expectations for the session. By breaking the ice as quickly as possible, you'll create a comfortable atmosphere that will improve everybody's experience.

Start connecting with your audience from your first word. Take a breath just before you open your mouth.

TRY THIS ■ *Look out on the audience and see the faces there not as opinions to be swayed but as people who want to do something meaningful with their lives as much as you do.*

Assume that your information and vision can be of real benefit to everyone in that room, and to the people touched by them. In words, tone, and style, be ready to transmit that you are a friend. You want to draw your audience in, as if you were talking in your own living room.

If you bring attitudes like these to your speech, your audience will pick them up, and that will help link them to you and your message. The benefits flow both ways; the more connected you feel to an audience, the more confident you'll be.

If your purpose is self-serving, on the other hand, you'll end up manipulating your audience instead of serving it. Your information and speaking skills might be wonderful, but you'll be less credible, or less enthusiastic, or less connected to your audience. Something will be off. And at least some people will notice this even if you don't.

AVOID THIS MISTAKE ■ *If you're new to public speaking, don't try to imitate some slick performer you've seen—audiences quickly sense faking.*

You'll have a far easier time connecting to your audience if you come across as a real, believable, caring person. As in any communication, be yourself, and that will be plenty good enough.

Finally, unless you're giving a paper on nuclear physics at Caltech, don't read your speech. It's fine to have notes in front of you. Even a verbatim text can work—but only if you read it through enough times beforehand so that your head is not constantly bobbing up and down, distracting your audience from connecting to the person behind the words. Of course, if you're the president of the United States, use the teleprompter.

Tell stories. Communicating a personal experience is a lot more powerful than communicating a concept. Make as many points as you can by telling your own story or, failing that, someone else's story that you know well. Telling people that a river is polluted is not as powerful as telling them that your kids got sick when they swam in it. People will be unlikely to join your service group just because you tell them there are 9,456 homeless people in your city. They're more likely to join if, in addition to your facts, you also tell them the story of

A GIRAFFE STORY
Sarri Gilman

Sarri Gilman will tell you, "We recycle cans better than these kids are treated." To Gilman, a social worker in Everett, Washington, "these kids" are the nation's homeless and abused kids with no safe place to go. She'll tell you about the 14-year-old girl with the six-month-old baby, neither of whom had slept in three days. Or Marcus, whose mom is dead and whose father is in jail. Or Lena, 16, abandoned by her mom at age 6 and left with an alcoholic father who abused her. Some experts say that on any given night there are half a million teenagers on the nation's streets.

Unlike many people who see homeless teens, Gilman didn't look the other way. For years she had worked with "at-risk" adolescents and knew how serious teen homelessness was in her community. She says, "I got tired of seeing the pain behind the eyes of these youngsters." Some of the kids had been thrown out by their families.

For Gilman, the last straw was the young girl who had been searching for her mom at local motels and ended up kidnapped, drugged with heroin, and raped by her mother's boyfriend. Gilman says, "It kept me awake at night trying to figure out what I could do to make a difference."

That "difference" became a miracle known as Cocoon House, a safe haven in Everett for teenagers in crisis. It's a

Joe Smith, who is living on the street and depending on handouts to survive.

Humor can be tricky. Use a warm-up joke if you must, but I've long felt that this tactic simply tells audience members that you've read some book on public speaking, and it can actually discourage them from connecting with you. On the other hand, funny stories and anecdotes in the flow of your speech—*especially if they are self-deprecating*—help engage people. If you know your audience well, poking good-natured fun at others can work, too.

Put your heart into it. Don't be shy to express your feelings and to evoke the feelings of people in your audience. My experience is that the more formal or bureaucratic the people in the audience are, the more they hunger for some personal touch, particularly if the issue is sensitive. I'm not talking about getting out the crying towel; I'm talking about honest, appropriate expressions of our common humanity. I gave a speech to a bunch of sophisticated Seattle lawyers awhile back, and I knew from the outset that it would be hard to bust through their professional reserve. So I left the podium and walked around the hotel ballroom with a handheld mike. I started by talking openly and with some humor about how I'd handled (or botched) some of the emotional and ethical risks I'd faced in my career as a Foreign Service Officer. One lawyer, then another, shared a personal story, and in 20 minutes people were talking about risks and meaning in their lives at a depth I'd say none of them had expected.

beautiful home that shelters kids age 13–18 for a night, a week, or even a few months while they get help locating a stable home. At Cocoon House, teenagers find safety, warmth, clean beds and clothes, toiletries, a living room, and a big yard. There's also a dinner table where kids eat together as a family, a first-time experience for some of them.

This "cocoon" was not spun overnight. When Gilman started, in 1991, she had no track record and no money, and was unknown in the community. Friends warned her that she'd go bankrupt. When she asked civic leaders for assistance, some of them denied that there was a problem. She was criticized for being "too optimistic," for having expectations of kids that were too high. But Gilman persisted. One city official said, "She went into this with a heart and a determination that most people don't have. This isn't a job for her, it's a mission."

Gilman persuaded the local Lions Club to buy the building that would become Cocoon House. She enlisted innumerable volunteers to help fix it up. She spent countless hours reaching out to businesses and social-services agencies. The harder Gilman worked, the more the community responded. But in spite of the increasing support, Gilman says that when the doors opened, Cocoon House had $15 in the bank.

■ *Show by your words and tone that you care for the people you're speaking to, and for their situation. Caring builds trust, and audiences are more likely to follow the lead of speakers they trust.*

Sometimes I'll pick out a few people in the audience and focus on them for a few seconds as if I were speaking to them alone. I can feel the links this creates, and it adds to my confidence that I can reach others—even that guy reading the newspaper in the sixth row.

Many people draw back from being personal or caring in public speaking. They overintellectualize, use abstract instead of personal examples, and avoid eye contact. Tactics like these communicate, all right—they say that such speakers are afraid or unwilling to give of themselves.

Describe the problem that concerns you with enough detail to show you've done your homework—but not so much that you lose the human connection.

AVOID THIS MISTAKE ■ *Don't use a lot of charts, overhead projections, or computer-assisted graphics.*

These things can be great for getting information across, but I find that too many speakers hide behind them to take the focus off themselves; the gizmos become a cop-out from making the personal connections that should be made. It's important for the audience to get the message from you, not from the graphics. It's your vision and your enthusiasm that are going to bring your listeners around,

A GIRAFFE STORY
continued

She never gave up, and Cocoon House not only survived its modest beginning, but it grew. Thanks to the Washington State Department of Community Development and other concerned supporters, financing became more stable. Soon after establishing Cocoon House, Gilman started planning Cocoon Complex, a converted motel that today houses two dozen young people who can stay for one month to three years, many of them working in a nonprofit restaurant that the kids run themselves while they finish school, save money, and, most important, heal.

Cocoon House newsletters note that 81 percent of Cocoon kids move to stable housing within 24 months, 50 percent of eligible ones find jobs, and 60 percent earn a diploma or a GED. Beyond the statistics are hundreds of stories of tired, scared, and abused teenagers who got a chance for a better life.

Recently Cocoon House heard from one such former resident. He's now 20, employed by a software company, and sharing a house with friends. He ends his letter with, "Sarri, thank you for believing in me, and for opening your heart to so many others whose lives would be wasted without the dream that you made happen."

Web link: Cocoon House (www.cocoonhouse.org).

not the pictures and charts. If you have a lot of technical data, include it as handouts so that you only have to summarize it in your presentation.

Create a vision—a clear, concrete picture of the results you want the audience to see. Make the vision big enough—make the stretch exciting.

A Large Midwest Health-Care Firm

Before speaking to the officers of a large Midwest health-care firm, I read a statement of its founding vision—a very idealistic statement about healing and service that ended, "Our mission and values will radiate throughout our health care ministry." Pressured to cut costs, however, the firm had recently watched as the nursing resources it could devote to delivering the kind of care described in its vision became fewer and fewer.

I took the group back to that founding vision. "Three years from now," I asked, "when your mission and values are 'radiating throughout your health-care ministry,' what, specifically, is radiating? Are you another casualty of corporate greed—or something else? What do you see happening for your patients and for yourselves?"

My goal was to lead these people back to the pictures of personal and compassionate service the company had been founded on—pictures that had drawn most of them to work there in the first place. As I'd hoped, there was such power in those pictures that it has since helped energize the company to fight to keep them real.

Describe your own personal involvement and commitment. If you're asking people to get involved in a project, tell them first about your own involvement. Your request will be more credible if people know you're not just talk.

Provide a summary. Hearing a presentation is not like reading a book or a magazine; listeners can't go back and look up a point they missed. So recap your main points shortly before you finish. If there are many points or a lot of technical data, put supporting materials on a table and tell people they can pick up a copy on the way out. *Don't* hand out the materials beforehand, or some people will be reading them when they should be listening to you.

Q & A's. If there's time to answer questions after your presentation, offer to do so. Q & A's are a good opportunity to clear up anything that your audience may not have understood or that was incomplete, to make points you wish you'd made, and to reinforce your central message.

Participatory sessions. If your presentation is participatory, such as a workshop, make it as active and spontaneous as you can. Be attuned to what's going on in the room. Show real interest in the concerns and questions that people raise, and follow up on them. Let participants help set the agenda: What information turned out to be unnecessary? What points have been raised that you hadn't planned to address but now should?

If your presentation is a training session, never talk down to audience members out of your superior knowledge—the point is not to have them anoint you as an authority but to excite them with the knowledge you're giving them and to empower them as learners. Unless your presentation is about techniques that must be done precisely, such as administering CPR, don't worry about nailing down every angle in the first pass. In fact, it's often a good idea to leave time and space for people to wonder, to ponder the unknowns, and then to ask questions.

Know you've done your best. If you've prepared well, if you've given of yourself, you can expect to succeed. And keep in mind that nobody pleases everybody every time. I've had people in the same audience tell me that I spoke too long and not long enough, and that the same joke was wonderfully funny and that it fell flat. I can give what I think is the best speech of my life and there will always be at least one feedback sheet that says I was a waste of time. And I'm a pro.

TIPS FOR RAISING MONEY

Asking people to support your cause with money is a form of communication, and how well you do at it will depend on how persuasive you are in getting your message through. What you've read so far in this chapter will help you in raising money face-to-face or in public presentations.

There are already many excellent books on fund-raising, and I note a few of them in the "Resources" section at the end of the book. What follows are additional tips that—from my own experience in raising money for more than 20 years—I know are important yet given too little attention:

▪ Have a Positive Mind-Set around Asking for Money

I hear people say, "I hate to beg for money." *You are not begging!!* You are giving people an opportunity to participate in something you believe in—something that will improve the world, or at least your part of it. You, the activist, and they, the funders, are partners and peers, and you should act that way. It took a while, but Giraffe Sarri Gilman finally got her community to see it that way (see sidebar, page 128).

▪ First Tap the Wallets Closest to Home

There's no more powerful tool in fund-raising than a personal relationship, so start with the people you already know—your extended family, your friends, and your acquaintances. Go through your card file (or its electronic equivalent). Ask others working with you to do the same. Since you're not approaching these prospective donors as a stranger, the "ask" is simple: just describe what you're doing and why it's important, and ask for help.

▪ Carefully Prepare for Meetings with Potential Major Donors

Get as much biographical information about donors as you can beforehand, including their giving history—ask mutual friends, search the Internet, and/or look up the person in published sources such as *Who's Who*.

Tailor your presentation for each potential major donor, stressing the elements of your program likely to be of most interest to that person, and using the skills and sensitivities described in the first part of this chapter. Be ready to answer direct questions about mission, goals, and budgets. Make sure your vision of end results is crisp and compelling. Ask for an amount of money appropriate to that person. Have a good answer to the question, "What happens if this project is not funded?"

While you should send or leave behind written materials on your cause with a prospective major donor, you shouldn't rely too much on paper to make your case. What you really want is to establish a personal relationship with the person that will result in long-term support for your cause. That can only be done in person. Once major donors are on board, you need to cultivate them—for example, by sending them special mailings and notices, inviting them to thank-you events, and generally keeping in contact on a regular basis.

■ Learn How to Write Persuasive Fund-Raising Letters

In your letter, answer these questions, more or less in this order:

- *What's the problem your group is taking on?*

- *Why should the reader care about it—why should he or she read on?*

- *What's your clear, sharp vision of how things look with the problem solved?*

- *What's your plan for helping solve the problem/attain the vision?*

- *Why will your plan work, and why are you competent to solve the problem?*

- *How much money do you need?*

- *How, specifically, will the reader's contribution be used?*

- *What will happen if this problem is not solved?*

Identify key support you already have. People's decisions on whether or not to give to a cause are often based on their recognition of other people who are already connected to that cause. So your letter needs to demonstrate the support you've already gained. Send your message on letterhead that lists your board of directors and/or advisers if you have them. Say how much you've already raised, for this or similar projects. Mention that you've contributed, and say how much your board has given, if you have a board. If possible, arrange for a challenge grant from a major donor beforehand so that you can tell readers their gifts will be matched dollar for dollar, two for one, or whatever the terms of the challenge might be.

Reach people's hearts while you convince their heads. I almost never give to an appeal that is composed of one emotional picture after another, because I don't trust that the senders are hard-edged enough to solve the problem. On the other hand, logic and data alone are rarely enough to move me to give. Like most people, I look for emotion *and* competence.

Keep this balance. Give enough details of your plan and your history to show people that you know what you're doing. But be personal and open in describing how this issue affects you and why you are involved. Tell stories of people affected by the problem and by your group's work to solve it. Make the stories as personal and compelling as you can. Enclose a few pictures and/or press clips, and perhaps an eye-catching brochure.

▪ Apply to Foundations; They Are Often the Source of the Largest Gifts

Make every effort to develop a personal contact at a foundation. Do this before you ever start writing a proposal. Go through a friend who already has a contact; failing that, do it cold. If the foundation is local, seek an appointment with an appropriate person about your request. If it's not local, then ask to speak to that person on the phone.

KEY POINT ▪ *The odds of getting a foundation grant at least triple if you can address your proposal to someone who knows your name and the sound of your voice.*

It's even possible to get staff at foundations so interested in your project that they'll coach you on what they think you should emphasize to win over the decision makers.

Follow directions. Whether or not you think a foundation's requirements are relevant, follow the directions on its forms precisely; the competition for grants is fierce, and all a foundation needs is one small excuse to take you out of the running.

Set a light tone; that will help your proposal stand out. In general, foundation proposals tend to be more formal in tone and style than direct-mail letters. But don't get swept up in formality just because the instructions make it sound as if the foundation wants a senior thesis. Try to put yourself in the proposal reader's shoes. A little informality and humor can be powerful—picture yourself as a bleary-eyed foundation executive who has been reading stodgy, academic prose for six hours and will be delighted to see a request that has some life in it.

Follow up. Of course you know to send a thank-you letter if you get a grant. But it's also important to acknowledge any turn-down letter that's more than a form. Send back a note thanking the signer for the foundation's consideration. She'll remember that courtesy if you apply again; in such a competitive business, that edge might be all that's needed to put you ahead of another competitor in the next round.

If you've made a personal contact during the application process, call that contact to thank him or her for working with you, even if you were unsuccessful. Ask for any advice that might make your request more compelling the next time around, or with other donors. I find that most foundation staffers are helpful, and that these post-mortem calls often produce usable feedback.

PLAY IT AGAIN

- *Persuasive communications require style, attitude, heart, and vision:*
  - *Know how you come across to others—and adjust if you have to.*
  - *Stay as personal and informal as you can.*
  - *Communicate a vision—a compelling, hopeful, achievable picture of future possibilities.*
  - *Listen. The more sensitive you are to the person you're talking to, the more effectively you'll shape and deliver your own messages.*
  - *Be conscious of the little things.*
  - *Don't send mixed messages.*

WHAT'S NEXT?
It's in your interest to spread the word about your project, both to enlist support from other people and to encourage them to follow your lead. The next chapter is about public relations and media.

- How to give a great speech:
  - Don't worry. You are not the point of the speech—your message is the point. Focus on getting that message across and you'll lessen your concerns about yourself.
  - Before you start:
    — Fulfill the bill. Be absolutely sure that you and the sponsors of the event are on the same page regarding the theme of your speech.

    — Know your subject—and your audience.

    — Make an outline of what you want to say.

    — Reflect on the importance of what you're about to do. Take responsibility for the impact on each person of what you're about to say.

    — Anticipate good results.
  - When the presentation starts:
    — Take control of the introduction.

    — Start connecting with your audience from your first word.

    — Tell stories.

    — Put your heart into it. Don't be shy about expressing your feelings and evoking the feelings of people in your audience.

    — Create a vision. Make the vision big enough—make the stretch exciting.

    — Describe your own personal involvement and commitment.

    — Provide a summary.
- Tips for raising money:
  - Have a positive mind-set around asking for money.
  - First tap the wallets closest to home.
  - Carefully prepare for meetings with potential major donors.
  - Learn how to write killer fund-raising letters. Reach people's hearts while you convince their heads.
  - In foundation fund-raising:
    — Make every effort to develop a personal contact at a foundation.

    — Follow directions.

    — Set a light tone; that will help your proposal stand out.

    — Send thank-you letters for rejections as well as approvals.

CHAPTER NINE

*The good you do isn't going to be replicated unless you let others
know about it. Publicity isn't about anybody's ego. It's about
getting more people to do what you've done.*
ANN MEDLOCK,
Founder of the Giraffe Heroes Project

DEALING WITH THE MEDIA:
THE SECRETS OF GOOD PR

*Thanks and a tip of the hat to Ann Medlock, founder of the Giraffe Heroes Project
and veteran publicist, for many of the ideas and suggestions in this chapter.*

THIS CHAPTER is about using media to advance your cause. By
"media" I mean primarily public media such as newspapers, television, and radio. But there's also media that you can create yourself—
speeches, Web sites, flyers, brochures, posters, and newsletters. All
media act like megaphones: they amplify your message and get it to
lots of people at once.

WHY SHOULD YOU TELL PEOPLE
WHAT YOU'RE DOING?

The first reason for telling your story is a practical one:

KEY POINT ■ *The more that people know about your project, the more
support you'll attract, including volunteers and money. If your project
involves public education—that is, you want people to change their attitude
or behavior in some way—using media is crucial for getting your idea across.*

Also, good deeds multiply when other people know about them.
Whether or not you need help, telling the story of your project
through media can prompt others to follow your example. When

you look at it that way, you've got an obligation to publicize the work you're doing as an active citizen—put it out there so that it can multiply!

CREATING A MEDIA STRATEGY

Having a well-thought-out media strategy as part of your action plan (see chapter 5) not only will help you bring your project to the attention of the media, but it will also keep your messages focused and coordinated with each other, and consistent with your overall vision and action plan. Having a media strategy and keeping it in mind will increase your confidence in dealing with media and will make it less likely that you'll be pulled off mission by the stress and chaos that often accompany broadcast or print coverage. Finally, having a media strategy increases the chances that reporters and editors will get your story right—though even the best work on your part is no guarantee that they won't make some mistakes.

A media strategy answers these basic questions:

- *What's your story—and how do you get media to tell it?*

- *What media assets do you have or can you easily get—such as writers, speakers, artists, graphic designers, and Web techies?*

- *What kinds of media will work best for your project?*

- *What do you need to do, and when, to get the media results you want?*

■ What's Your Story?

Most broadcasts and newspapers lead with so-called hard news—timely, breaking (and usually bad) news. Then they proceed to "soft" news—less urgent stuff that won't make the front page or the top of a newscast but might be a good story for the inside of the paper or the later parts of a newscast. Hard news always gets priority in terms of resources too, so the "harder" your story is, the more likely you are to get covered, especially on a busy news day. If it's been a big day for crises in your community and around the world, the opening of a literacy tutoring program probably won't get reporters on-site, but a project with some dramatic action might, as in "Community Group Blocks Bulldozers Filling Wetland."

Hard news or soft, *focus on the most interesting aspects of what you're doing.* Does it involve community members in an unusually creative way? Does it touch on an issue already in the news? Are there ethnic or generational elements that will be interesting to important subsets of readers/viewers?

KEY POINT ■ *Being different attracts media attention.*

The Giraffe Heroes Project, for example, puts bold red giraffes on everything and calls people who stick their necks out "Giraffes" as a playful way of getting attention. Once we've got that attention, we can talk about the serious issues motivating our work. Giraffe Granny D was an 89-year-old with arthritis and emphysema who walked across the country to publicize her cause. Now *that* was different (see sidebar on this page).

A story is also more likely to attract media if it involves events and actions that could be videotaped or photographed. Launch events and completion events, like ribbon cuttings and celebrations of success, are possibilities, especially if you get a VIP to be part of the event. Known names attract media, and this attraction works both ways—VIPs will be more likely to come if they know that media will be invited. Keep in mind that if you

A GIRAFFE STORY
Doris Haddock

There's nothing unusual about taking a walk. But if you're 89 years old and you have arthritis and emphysema, you wear a steel back brace, and your "walk" is a 3,200-mile cross-country political statement, then it's amazing.

Doris Haddock (better known as Granny D) is a former executive secretary and lifetime political activist who is not taking retirement sitting down. She's concerned over the role of campaign contributions in determining the outcome of political elections and therefore the direction of our democracy.

Her civics discussion group in Peterborough, New Hampshire, started a petition drive to persuade Congress to pass a campaign-finance-reform bill. Many politicians ignored this issue or actually said it was unimportant. Haddock concluded that a petition would not be enough, that she needed to do something dramatic to help rescue our democracy "from this sewer of cash and greed we've slipped into."

That something dramatic was her decision to "walk the talk" and travel, on foot, across the United States talking to people about influence peddlers who've "set up their cash registers in our temple of democracy." She trained hard for her marathon journey, hiking almost every day wearing a 25-pound backpack. Family want luminaries to attend your event, you have to invite them far in advance.

■ What Media Assets Do You Have or Can You Easily Get?

The answer to this question will impact your media strategy, including your choice of which media to use. The assets you're looking for include writing, speaking, artistic and graphic-design capabilities, and technical expertise with Web sites.

■ What Kinds of Media Will Work Best for Your Project?

That depends on whom you want to know about your project and when you want them to know it:

Newsletters and Web sites. If your project has a mailing list, then a print newsletter is still a good way of getting basic information out to supporters. These days, however, newsletters are increasingly sent out online or replaced altogether by Web sites.

Creating a Web site is a quick and relatively cheap way to present news of your work to large numbers of people and to invite their support—especially if your project is national or global. Successful sites don't have to be fancy, but they must be attractive, informative, and user-friendly. Giraffe Karen Storek uses a state-of-the-art Web site with downloadable audio and video messages (see sidebar, page 148). Our experience at the Giraffe Heroes Project is that it's worth spending

A GIRAFFE STORY
continued

members tried to talk her out of it, but she went right ahead, setting out from California in January 1999 and heading for Washington, D.C.

She logged 10 miles a day through sandstorms, blizzards, blistering heat, and torrential rains. She braved danger and even death each day she walked. She was hospitalized for dehydration after crossing the Mojave Desert and risked hypothermia by skiing through snow in Maryland. Her emphysema made her lungs "sound like a teakettle" when she marched up a hill, but she kept walking.

And everywhere she walked, she talked. She told people all across the country that "fundraising muscle should not be the measure of a candidate" but that the candidate with the most money almost always wins. Often the winning candidate has over *ten times* as much money as the loser.

Haddock told people that the voice of the common citizen is drowned out by companies and associations that shower cash on political candidates and then expect the winner to pay them back by voting as those contributors want them to. She told her audiences that over $100 million *a month* floods into Washington, D.C., to influence politicians, adding, "You know where that leaves you and me, don't you?"

some time and money to get good professional help with Web site design.

The trick is to get people to visit your site amid the millions of sites now up.

TRY THIS ■ *Put your Web link on every piece of printed material you create for your project, include it in any speeches and interviews, and use e-mail messages to "push" people onto the site.*

Keep your site current. Posting regular updates takes effort, but a site that's clearly months out of date may do you more harm than good.

For more on Web sites, see "Resources," at the end of the book.

Magazines. Magazine stories are more permanent than those in newspapers or electronic media. They can have a focus from local to international, but magazine stories take months to process, so they are not much good if you need immediate attention or support. If your project is long-term, however, a good magazine article about it, photocopied and wisely distributed, can be invaluable PR.

Newspapers, television, and radio. It's far easier to get a story placed in a newspaper than in a magazine, especially if the story is local. Television is best for attracting attention, especially if you have a lot of interesting visuals. With time per story generally limited to a few minutes or less, however, TV is not a good way to explain a complicated program. Don't forget radio—it usually gives you a lot more time than

A GIRAFFE STORY
continued

Along the way, Granny D met a lot of people, many of whom were so impressed that they started walking with her. She says that of everyone she encountered along the way, not one believed that "their voice as an equal citizen" counted for much in government.

Haddock preached in churches, gave speeches, joined in parades, and appeared in newspapers and on radio and television. One of her admirers said that she motivated "tens of thousands of young people to get involved in civic life, and has inspired older people to stay involved in their communities."

Fourteen months, 12 states, and 3,200 miles later, Granny D arrived in Washington, D.C. She had celebrated her 90th birthday on the road. Others might have taken a long rest after such a journey, but within days Haddock was arrested with 30 others for demonstrating in the U.S. Capitol building. Her "crime" was reading the Declaration of Independence on the Capitol steps, telling people that we need now to declare "our independence from the corrupting bonds of big money in our election campaigns."

The judge could have given Granny D six months in prison and ordered her to pay a $500 fine. Instead, he imposed no jail time and told her, "Take

TV, and many people listen to drive-time radio and to radio call-in and talk shows.

Posters and flyers. These options can have a big impact at little cost, *if* your project is focused in a relatively small geographic area. Posters and flyers are visual media; they must grab someone's attention quickly and convey a single, simple message, such as a notice of an event.

Brochures. Brochures can hold more information than posters or flyers, and they are particularly useful as handouts at events and as attachments to mailings. They are still largely visual media, however; too many words and tightly crowded type can doom a brochure to go unread.

HOW TO GET THE MEDIA RESULTS YOU WANT

AVOID THIS MISTAKE ■ *Media coverage doesn't happen magically, so don't think that just because what you're doing is incredibly great, public media will hear about it and rush to tell your story.*

A GIRAFFE STORY
continued

care, because it's people like you who will help America reach our destiny." She went right back to the Capitol building and read the Bill of Rights. Yes—she was arrested again.

After her cross-country trek, Doris Haddock helped found the Free Democracy Movement, whose purpose is to raise the volume of individual citizens' voices. Partly prompted by her courageous efforts, several states are reforming their campaign-finance laws, and the issue now has a much higher profile among voters. In the words of one U.S. senator, "She's rebuilt our faith in the idea that one person can make a difference."

Granny D is still going strong; she ran for the U.S. Senate in New Hampshire in 2004.

Web link: Doris Granny D Haddock (www.grannyd.com).

Sometimes that can happen—a curious reporter may track you down and the next thing you know, your project is in the paper and on TV. But that's not usually the way it works. Stories don't just appear on TV and radio and in newspapers—somebody alerted the stations or papers—so you'll probably have to make some moves to get media to tell your story. One way to do this is by sending a *press release*.

■ Writing a Press Release

A press release is a short description of an action or event that is faxed, mailed, or e-mailed to newspapers and to television and radio stations. Press releases can describe something that's just happened, or they can invite reporters to an event that's about to happen. They can focus on a milestone or give other information about an ongoing effort.

Sending a press release doesn't guarantee that media will respond. There are many competing stories, and yours may well get ignored or lost—there's a black hole in newsrooms that can suck in press releases, never to be seen again.

Still, if you *don't* send a release (and make follow-up calls), the media definitely won't know what you're doing and there won't be any coverage, and that means no community awareness of the great things you're doing, no support coming forth from the community to help you get the job done, and no chance of contagious replication of your efforts by others. It's worth the effort to create and send the release.

In writing a press release, use the journalistic style a reporter would use so the editor will see that the story is ready to use, with little or no work. Press releases, like news stories, are usually written with the most important information first and the least important last. This allows editors to cut the piece from the bottom up if they need to shorten it, without deleting vital information. Your task is to make the editor's job as easy as possible, which increases the chances of the release being used. Here's how to write a good release:

- *Use eye-catching letterhead; you can use your computer to create the template. You want the reporter or editor to immediately recognize the release as coming from your group—and to be able to find it easily in his stack of releases when you make your follow-up call.*

- *Double-space your release, and leave fairly wide margins on the sides for editors to write in.*

- *Keep it short; one page is best, two is max. You can send more information if and when a reporter shows interest.*

- *Put a release date at the top and at least one name and number that reporters can call for more information.*

- *Open with answers to "Who, what, when, where, and why?"*

- *Don't exaggerate.*

- Include good quotes from other people in your release, giving their names and saying who they are. Don't praise or otherwise evaluate your action yourself in the release.

- Keep attached background materials to a minimum—perhaps a fact sheet or frequently asked questions (FAQ).

See the sample press release on page 146. It's written to be sent *after* an event. A different release could also have been sent *before* the event, encouraging media people to come and see it for themselves (see "Timing a Press Release," later in this chapter).

■ Targeting a Press Release

At large newspapers, different kinds of stories are handled by different people, so before you send anything, think creatively about your story and who might naturally be interested. Target your releases to the editor or writer most likely to use your story. The more angles you can think of, the greater your chances of getting coverage. Hard news is the domain of the *city desk*, so activists who are planning to dramatize their issue with a public protest would contact the city editor. A story on helping save a wetland should interest an environmental reporter. A story on helping the homeless goes to the community-affairs person or people.

A good way to find the right people to contact is to get a current media directory at the public library. There are several national directories that might include contacts in your area, and most major cities have a citywide directory. Many directories go into useful detail about who covers what. Reading the papers you are interested in will also help you become familiar with who covers what, and which reporters are likely to be more interested in covering your story.

At small newspapers, simply contact the editor with any story. At small television and radio stations, call the program director to ask who the proper person is. At larger stations, the assignment editor can tell you whom you should call. For radio, talk to the news director (unless it's a very large station, in which case you should call the front desk to ask who the proper person is). Finally, you can sometimes get good information on staffing from the Web sites of local media companies. But the turnover in media jobs can be fast. Make

SMITHVILLE UNITED
Citizens making our town better
www.bergville.org   456-7890

For release: Noon, Monday, June 13, 2005
For more information call: Dudley Doright 360-330-4476

MAYOR OPENS STUDENT-DESIGNED HOUSING
Tent City Homeless Move In

This morning, Mayor Andrea DeVega and City Housing Director Forrest Watkins rolled out a red carpet for the first occupants of Morrison Estates, a new low-cost-housing development at the corner of Lenwood and Houston streets. The 15 families moved to the new development from Tent City, the homeless encampment on the grounds of the Public Gardens. Morrison Estates was designed by seven Smithville State architecture students. They were enlisted in the program by Smithville United, a local citizens' group that promotes community redevelopment projects.

Smithville United persuaded the Maralex Corporation to donate land for the project and solicited other local businesses for the construction funds. The group also enlisted the help of social workers at the South Side Clinic to find suitable candidates to live in Morrison Estates. All tenants are mandated to find employment and begin making the modest mortgage payments within six months of moving in. Clinic staff will work with the tenants to assist them in meeting this goal.

Mayor DeVega said this morning, "Morrison Estates is a marvel of creative thinking. It will help many of our city's homeless and, I hope, be a model and inspiration for other neighborhoods. I congratulate Smithville United, Smithville State, the Smithville business community, and the South Side Clinic."

Seven Smithville State architecture students spent an academic year designing Morrison Estates, working with Tent City residents to be sure their designs met future residents' needs. They were inspired by the work of Habitat for Humanity, a nonprofit organization that builds affordable housing for the poor.

Smithville United's president, Charlene Pyle, told the opening-day crowd, "It was great to see people of many ages and interests, from so many sectors of the city, working together to create these houses. Smithville should take a bow today."

#

phone calls to verify that the people you want to reach are still there. If they aren't, ask who has replaced them.

You can send your press release to any and all of the media people mentioned above, but once a reporter responds, don't then offer it to another one at the same paper or station. You don't want to set up a crossfire between them. The only decent thing to do is to work with the first reporter who responds from that paper or station, even if that's the weekly education columnist and you really wanted their hottest daily reporter.

■ Timing a Press Release

If your group needs public support as soon as possible, create a kickoff event with some attractive visuals, and seek coverage from local newspapers and especially television. Word your press release in a way that invites reporters to come to this event that has not yet happened. That's still no guarantee that the reporter won't stay at her desk and write her story from your release, so be sure that your release covers the points you want to make.

All media have deadlines. If you want coverage for a particular date and time, you should check with any media you're considering to verify their cutoff times. Deadlines for radio vary widely. For a morning newspaper, the deadline is probably midnight the night before. For afternoon papers it's anywhere from 8 a.m. to noon. For weeklies it might be 24 hours (or more) in advance. For television, if they're not going live, the footage has to be in at least two hours before airtime.

■ Following Up a Press Release

If you've sent out press releases, follow them up in a few days with phone calls. Have a copy of the release in hand and be ready to talk it through for the person who sort of remembers seeing it, never laid eyes on it, or saw it but lost it—remember that black hole. Have something new to add to the story; that will give you a "hook" to hang your call on. For example: "I wanted you to know that the governor has just commended Smithville for that new housing project we wrote you about."

In all phone work with media, be ready for anything: If the person you're talking to isn't interested, you can pitch the story from a new angle. If *that* doesn't work, ask who else on staff *would* be interested. If you get a lead this way, call that person and be sure to tell him that so-and-so thought he'd be interested.

■ Getting Professionals to Help You

Whenever you can, enlist other people's paid PR professionals to help you get the word out. If you invited a VIP to your media event and led the press release with her role, that gives you a chance to enlist the VIP's publicist in getting reporters to cover the story. That's not the only reason to invite the VIP—her presence also helps reporters to see the importance of the event and shows the significance of your program. If other large organizations—such as universities, hospitals, or major businesses—are involved in your activity or event, try to get their press offices involved.

There's help available at PR agencies. Especially if someone in your group has the contacts to pull it off, such agencies can sometimes detail staffers to do pro bono work for causes.

■ Providing Backup

Even on a heavy news day, you still have a chance for airtime or print space if you're willing to do the media's job for them. You can, for example, use a high-quality video camera to shoot the event and then get that footage to a television station quickly, as a video press release. If your group has members with the skills and equipment to do that, they should call

In 1988 Karen Storek had a baby—and a great idea: gather and distribute simple, meaningful parenting advice, make it readily accessible and simple for anyone to understand, and make it all free. As a new mother, Storek had been frustrated by the difficulty of obtaining vital information. Although it existed, it wasn't in one place, and it could be overwhelming for a new parent to collect and organize. Storek realized that, especially with new parents, a single piece of information could mean the difference between life and death for a child.

Storek established a nonprofit called the New Parents Network (NPN) and began by creating packets to distribute in hospitals in Tucson, Arizona. They contained information on product recalls, poisonous plants, child-care resources, immunization schedules, abuse prevention, and nutrition.

Storek knows there's no money in serving the poor, but she refused to stray from her mission to help "those most in need and hardest to reach." NPN materials were neutral, noncommercial, nonpolitical, and nonreligious, with no agenda other than promoting children's health and safety. In the beginning Storek worked endless hours for little pay as NPN's sole employee, selling personal valuables and going into debt to keep it viable. Some people tried to get her local stations and ask about their policies and standards for such footage.

For newspapers, you can do your own still photos (or hire a professional to do them) and submit them with a post-event press release. This is a good idea whether or not you get coverage. Photos taken by media belong to them and can't be used without permission. By taking your own photos, you ensure that you'll have good illustrations for your own use. Video footage you take yourself can be used later on to create your own video programs, without your having to worry about copyrights and royalties.

Remember—pictures of people in action are more likely to be used. Go for shots of people doing something that tells the story.

■ Preparing for On-Site Coverage

OK, your press releases have succeeded. The media are coming. Now—well before a photographer or a TV cameraperson arrives—you have to come through on what you promised they'd see.

KEY POINT ■ *First, to get good newspaper photographs or television footage, something visual has to be going on.*

People talking on phones or reading are boring. So is a shot of one person handing another a piece of paper.

Review your options for an action shot. Then think of some background or props that help tell the story. For example, the housing program described in the sample press release above might use a shot of the

A GIRAFFE STORY
continued

to throw in the towel, or at least to make NPN a for-profit operation. But Storek has never wavered from her calling. "I have learned not to give up," she says.

Storek draws together information from existing social-services and government agencies worldwide. In 1991, at the beginning of the Internet revolution, she set up an electronic bulletin board so that such organizations could submit simple, universally needed parenting information to NPN. Thousands of parents and professionals used the service, and NPN was acknowledged for its creative and innovative use of technology to benefit the common good.

In 1994 Storek was determined to reach more parents in Tucson who couldn't afford computers. She led a team to create software for interactive kiosks strategically located in low-income clinics. The kiosks printed out parenting messages with easy-to-understand text, photos, and graphics. In 2000 she upgraded the technology to a multilingual Web site. All over the world, midwives and public-health nurses serving the poor can access a wealth of practical parenting advice at the site. Radio stations can download audio from NPN, and television stations can access streaming video for public-service announcements that reach thousands of people.

mayor giving Tent City folks the keys to their new homes, taken in front of a sign for Morrison Estates. Or how about the mayor having a cup of coffee with some happy new residents in their shiny new kitchen?

A TV camera roams around shooting the B-roll. (A-roll is the main event, the key interviews; B-roll is the visuals that run under the reporter's voice, setting the mood and giving a visual background to the story.) Clean up visually distracting clutter and then strategically place posters, pictures, charts, or other visuals that will help you get your message across. In the event described in our sample press release, a large, colorful map of the area, and perhaps before-and-after photographs on a wall, could provide good B-roll.

While the best reporters and camerapeople won't need much guidance, it's still a good idea to point out your visuals when they arrive. You'll be helping them to do a good job quickly.

We're interviewed often at the Giraffe Heroes Project office. So we have a 4-by-4-foot collage of newspaper stories about Giraffes, a large wall map with pins showing where we've found Giraffes, giraffe posters, and a life-size papier-mâché giraffe. We also have our computer screens set to different pages of our Web site. Cameras head for these visuals every time.

A GIRAFFE STORY
continued

Today Storek is focused on the promise of the future, not the hardship of the past. "We're on the brink of a quantum leap," she says. "I believe that NPN will become a window into the largest collection of parenting information anywhere. We will become a global force to help parents around the world."

Web link: New Parents Network (www. newparentsnetwork.org).

▪ Giving an Interview or Holding a Press Conference

A newspaper or broadcast station may respond to your press release by assigning a reporter to interview you about it. If your project has already caught the media's attention, however, and something dramatic in it has happened or is about to happen, you can get your message to many reporters at once by inviting them to a press conference at a place of your choosing.

Most journalists run on crowded, high-pressure schedules, so you can expect them to be direct and moving fast. Still, they have as much at stake in having the interview or press conference succeed as you do—they want to relay the news in an interesting way, and they know they need your help to do that. You'll do fine at an interview or press conference if you remember a few basic tips:

Make sure that you're prepared. Review the vision for your project, your overall plan, and your media strategy before the interview. Think through this particular media opportunity and decide on the key points you want to get across.

Assemble any backup information you might need, such as charts and pictures. For a press conference, you'll probably want to prepare and hand to each reporter a *press kit*, which includes the original press release, fact sheet(s), and a *backgrounder*, or narrative history of your group and of this project. Reporters are always in a hurry, and you want to reduce the amount of time they have to spend taking notes so that they'll focus on the event and on what you're telling them. You'll add to your credibility if you include in your press kit other articles that have been done on your program. Media people need reassurance that others think it's a good story, but not too many others—you don't want them to say that the story's been covered enough.

If you're going to be on TV or radio, practice getting your key points across in short, to-the-point sentences. Remember that broadcast time is short and a rambling interview won't be used. Role-play with a friend, or record your key points and play them back to see if you're on the mark. Refine your answers. Be clear.

Keep the interview or press conference focused on your issue—and be prepared for anything. Reporters may well show up with interesting and relevant questions, but there's no guarantee that'll be the case. Sometimes a reporter will not have done his homework or will have no real interest in your project. He may also have several stories to do that day and be tired or distracted. So it's important for you to be single-minded about getting your point across.

Be polite but assertive. Don't wait for questions from the reporter to make your key points, and don't let yourself be sidetracked by irrelevant or even hostile questions. You can amiably steer the dialogue by saying things like, "Well, that's a very interesting point, but what's most unique about this project is . . ." As long as *you* are interesting, the reporter is likely to go along.

Communicate your vision. By now it should be sharply honed. The more clearly you're able to convey it, the better chance you have of getting reporters—and their audiences—excited about your project. You need to get all the relevant facts across, but when reporters begin to share your vision, they'll ask better questions and be more likely to write stories or do voice-overs that capture the excitement and importance of your project.

Be yourself. Take a deep breath, remember your main points, and don't try to imitate a pro—nobody expects you to be Diane Sawyer. The viewers, listeners, or readers will connect with you as the person you are. If you don't know the answer to a question, just say that you don't know but you'll find out.

AVOID THIS MISTAKE ■ *Don't ever assume that anything is "off the record." It probably isn't. And don't assume that the mike is off—it may not be.*

■ Following Up a Successful Media Event

When your story appears in the media, send the reporter who did the story a thank-you message. And now that you've made that contact, *cultivate* it. When you have an important new development, phone that reporter with a short update. If he or she doesn't want to do more about your program right now, ask who else might. Reporters who get familiar with your program (the contacts you've cultivated) may call you out of the blue when they're looking for a good story to do. Make sure you return their calls promptly—you could get a story you haven't had to push for.

It's useful to spend time establishing and maintaining good personal relationships, not just with the reporters who cover your stories but also with the reporters' bosses. Reporters come and go, but the senior people are more likely to be in place for longer periods.

Activist Evelyn Schaeffer offers these tips:

> I always made sure reporters could contact me easily, and that I returned their calls promptly. I also called to let them know when they had done a good job on a story, something that really does happen fairly often. That way, if I had to call for a correction it wasn't so difficult.
>
> After a couple of years of this, reporters were calling me for background, and when I provided something in writing to help them out, as often as not I saw it in the paper because the reporters knew they could trust me to be accurate with information. I think this all goes along with what you are saying in this book is the core of citizen activism, which is dedication to working on a cause because it has real meaning to yourself and your community. And that is, I believe, the exact opposite of "spin." Of course I wanted our facts and our issues and our proposals out in the public, but I wanted them fairly and honestly and truthfully presented, too. And as reporters compared what they saw and heard with my press releases and handouts over a period of time, our group gained credibility as a reliable news source—which made it much more likely that our news would be published.

Be sure to get copies of media coverage. Tape the broadcasts and clip the newspapers. Not everybody will see the story when it runs—but they'll see it if you send them copies. Send tapes or photocopies to everyone you think should have them. Put your news clips in all subsequent press kits. This kind of follow-up not only will attract more media coverage, but it will also help other people follow your lead.

Keep an archive of all media coverage as a key part of the official record of what your group has done. That archive will be an invaluable quick reference when you need it, especially as months turn into years.

▪ Letters to the Editor, Op-Eds, and Talk Shows

Not everything in media is launched with a press release. The simplest and most direct way to get your story in print or on the air is to tell it yourself. The drawback is that self-generated information and opinion is often given less weight than "news" items delivered by a source that at least claims to be objective. Still, letters to the editor, op-ed pieces, and talk-show comments can reach a lot of people.

Letters to the editor. A letter to the editor can be sent on its own, but it's more powerful if sent in conjunction with a press release from your organization on the same subject. You can also add power to your letters by writing and sending them as elements of a coordinated letter campaign. As part of that campaign, decide on the topics you want to address in your letters and then create a schedule for sending them in, keyed to events relevant to your cause—for example, county hearings or school board meetings. If you're part of a group, parcel out the task of writing the letters; you don't want them all to come from the same writer or the paper will balk.

CASE STUDY Island County

In the Citizens' Coalition, we decided on a half-dozen topics we wanted to address in letters over a six-month period, keyed to the County Planning Commission hearings on subjects such as transportation, zoning, and water rights. Then we parceled out these letters to different members of our group to write, after the whole group had agreed on the general positions we wanted to take.

Limit your letter to the number of words allowed by the newspaper—or risk having it cut in ways you won't like. More people read letters to the editor than you think—especially in small towns or rural areas where there is limited radio and TV coverage.

Op-eds. These are guest editorials that usually appear on the page opposite the editorial page, but they are longer and more prominently placed than letters to the editor. You usually need to have some recognized expertise on the issue you are writing about to get an op-ed published. It also doesn't hurt to know somebody at the paper.

Talk shows and interview shows. I confess that I've never done it, but someday I'm going to call in to a radio talk show. The people who do get on are rewarded for their wait with a minute or two of free airtime and the chance to banter with a host (who may be clueless).

It's much better if you can get on a drive-time news and interview show on radio, or an evening interview show on radio or television, including public television and cable. Select the show you want to get on, and then contact the program director to explain why what you have to say is of wide public interest and to demonstrate that you would be an engaging guest. If you get on, prepare yourself for these events as you would for any media interview (see "Giving an Interview or Holding a Press Conference," earlier in this chapter).

PLAY IT AGAIN

WHAT'S NEXT?
Institutions and bureaucracies have plenty of power to affect our lives, so it's important to know how to work with them. The next chapter will show you how.

■ *Why media? The more that people know about your project, the more support you'll attract, such as volunteers and money. If your project involves public education, using media is a crucial way to get your ideas across.*

■ *Create a media strategy to help you bring your project to the attention of the media, to keep your messages focused and coordinated with each other, and to increase your confidence in dealing with media.*

■ *What's your story? Focus on the most interesting aspects of what you're doing. A story is also more likely to attract media if it involves events and actions that could be videotaped or photographed.*

■ *Inventory the media assets you have or can easily get. The assets you're looking for include writing, speaking, artistic and graphic-design capabilities, and technical expertise with Web sites.*

■ *Determine the kinds of media that will work best for your project. That will depend on whom you want to know about what you're doing and when you want them to know it.*

■ *Get media to tell your story by sending them a press release.*

- Increase your chances of airtime or print space by shooting your own video or still photos and giving them to the newspaper or TV station. Go for shots of people doing something that tells the story.

- Prepare carefully for on-site media coverage. Review options for action shots; think of some background or props that help tell the story.

- If you're giving an interview or holding a press conference, review the vision for your project, your overall plan, and your media strategy before the interview. Think through the key points you want to get across. Assemble any backup information you might need. Keep the interview or press conference focused on your issue—and be prepared for anything.

- Follow up a successful media event by maintaining good relationships with the reporters who covered it.

- Try letters to the editor, op-eds, and talk shows.

*I think the question anyone has to ask is, "How will
I feel in six months if I don't do this now?"*
EVELYN SCHAEFFER,
Veteran Activist

■

GETTING INSTITUTIONS
TO DO WHAT YOU WANT

IF YOU WANT to solve a problem in the public realm, you're
almost certain to interact with institutions, especially government
and corporate ones. That's true whether you want to appeal your
tax bill, stop the cutting of old-growth timber, or improve transportation planning for your city.

Dealing with institutions and the people who run them is not
always an easy or pleasant process. This chapter covers three tools
for getting institutions to do what you want:

■ *developing the public will*

■ *working with "the System"*

■ *lobbying*

Chapter 11 covers:

■ *public testimony*

■ *legal action*

To these tools you can add three already covered:

■ *negotiation (chapter 7)*

■ *communication and fund-raising (chapter 8)*

■ *media and PR (chapter 9)*

Not covered in this book: electoral politics. My experience is limited, and there are already many excellent guides. See "Resources," at the end of this book.

You're certain to be using more than one of these tools at a time. For example:

CASE STUDY Island County

At the peak of its efforts to help create a Comprehensive Plan for Island County, the Citizens' Coalition was negotiating with county officials, testifying at hearings, organizing public forums, fund-raising, getting one of our own elected to county office, managing several lawsuits, making public presentations, and guiding a PR strategy—all at the same time. We felt like that guy in the circus spinning plates on the ends of sticks.

What made it work for us was a solid plan, updated weekly (see chapter 5). In those weekly meetings, we sought to find ways in which each of those elements could support the others. Our fund-raising and electoral pitches tracked our public-education and media efforts, for example, while those efforts in turn focused on the issues we were negotiating or litigating at that time. Our negotiating, public testimony, and courtroom strategies were closely linked; litigation gave added weight to our negotiating positions, and the research developed for our public testimony and negotiations buttressed our legal arguments.

In our best moments we were like a machine, with its many parts running in unison.

KEY POINT ■ *The more plates you have spinning, the more important it is to coordinate them as part of an overall strategy for change.*

Now here's a closer look at three of the plates:

DEVELOPING THE PUBLIC WILL

Special thanks to David Mathews and Noelle McAfee for ideas in their booklet Community Politics *(the Kettering Foundation, 200 Commons Road, Dayton OH 45459-2799).*

Especially if the changes you seek from institutions are significant, you and your team will have more success to the extent that you can develop and bring to bear the power of the public will.

■ What's the "Public Will" and Why Is It Important?

The public will is the resolve of a community to pursue a certain set of actions based upon its deep sense of what best serves its collective well-being. By "community" I'm talking mostly in this chapter about the neighborhood, town, or city where you live, but the concept of the public will also applies to the nation and to the planet.

KEY POINT ■ *The public will is not the same as public opinion, and certainly not that transient opinion created by the manipulation of an electorate by clever politicians. Nor is the public will the result of taking a poll or calling for a show of hands.*

The public will is far more difficult to develop than opinions and polls, goes far deeper, and is far more lasting than both. Civil rights legislation, restrictions on smoking in public places, and taxing ourselves to pay for public schools and libraries are familiar manifestations of the public will.

The public will by definition is broad based; the process of developing it should involve not just the usual activists and opinion makers but others whose lives could be affected by the issue(s) at hand—including those who rarely participate in any public process.

The public will cannot be imposed from the top down. The community needs to be fully invested in developing and articulating its will. Your motives in developing the public will should go beyond simply convincing the public of your own point of view. No matter how fervently you oppose the stadium bond issue or want a design-review code adopted for your town, developing the public will on issues such as these requires communications *among* citizens and not just from the top down. If your own input into the process is effective, the community may well end up where you are, but the process is open and fluid, and the results often transcend anyone's initial agenda.

So why bother? Developing the public will is rarely an easy or rapid task, and the results may force some shifts in your own vision. Why not just try to convince people of what you want them to do? As we saw in chapter 9, swaying people's opinions through public education and PR can be an important element in creating change.

KEY POINT ■ *If you've got the public will behind you and your cause, it becomes an important source of leverage and a uniquely important tool for change.*

Opinions swayed by outside messages lack the staying power of conclusions that the community *knows* reflect what it wants at a deep and meaningful level. This persistence and depth give the public will significant power. Institutions and public officials are very aware of this; they know they must respond to the public will if they want to enjoy public support over the long term.

■ Developing the Public Will Sometimes Must Start with Basic Communication

In polarized situations, sometimes the first step is simply to bring people together around any common interest you can find:

CASE STUDY Carmel, California

Carmel is a beautiful seaside town whose downtown community, when I visited there in the late '80s, was pretty much rock-ribbed Republican. Living in the steep canyons just outside of town, however, was a "hippie" community whose political views were decidedly to the left. At the height of the Cold War, tempers flared between the two groups, and a couple of ugly shouting matches left responsible people on both sides wondering what they might do to at last create a respectful atmosphere between these two very different groups.

The situation became so tense that nobody had any confidence that just "talking it through" would work. So we thought of one issue on which both sides shared an interest—keeping Carmel beautiful.

We organized a "Clean Up, Fix Up" day, carried out by work parties, each one composed of volunteers from both groups. Part of the work was to paint the town's fire hydrants.

The designs on those hydrants got very creative and colorful. More important, that work day helped dissolve some stereotypes and generate some mutual respect. It didn't change any views on the Cold War—and it stopped short of developing the public will. But it did dampen the local "war" and at least nudged open the doors to communication on other issues.

■ Use Public Forums to Develop the Public Will

Public forums are direct descendants of the town meetings begun in this country more than 200 years ago. Anyone can convene a public forum, and the location can be anywhere from the high school gymnasium to your living room.

Public forums are not public debates or panel discussions by experts. The purpose of public forums is to encourage *lateral* communication in an impartial and open environment—one that encourages people to recognize their capacities, to work through choices of community values and purposes, and to set community directions on critical policy issues.

CASE STUDY Island County

The Citizens' Coalition in Island County made extensive use of public forums in our five-year experience of helping create a Comprehensive Plan for the county. We used flyers, newspaper notices, and even paid ads to bring people to public forums (no local radio or TV in Island County). When we could, we hosted forums jointly with our political opponents. This both ensured that we had a wider cross-section of opinion in the room and tended to put people on their best behavior—lessening the kinds of petty altercations and name-calling that normally kept many "neutral" people from showing up at public meetings. Once, we even invited the head of the opposition to chair the meeting.

At their best, our forums were an exercise in civic learning that helped us pave the way for the common-ground solutions we eventually did find to many of the disputed issues. We supported and supplemented the work of public forums with a variety of other public-education tools, such as speeches, newspaper articles, letters to the editor, and direct mail.

■ Developing the Public Will Involves More Than Generating Opinions

Developing the public will means making extra efforts to involve everybody, especially shy people who are not used to speaking up in public. It also means encouraging people to talk in ways that reveal the *values* behind their opinions. At the coalition's forums, for example, we explored questions such as these: *Why* should we go to all this trouble to protect a threatened species or the "rural character" of our area? *Why* were property rights important, too? *What* kind of a community did we want?

"Going deeper" also means helping people see connections between different views and reflect on the consequences of different options. To do this requires community dialogue that is shared, reflective, and deliberate—one that allows even hidden facts, restraints, and connections to be identified and dealt with. Getting people to spend the time and effort (and often take the risks) to move beyond opinions to this level of dialogue takes time. When it happens, however, problems tend to get redefined—and that often leads to a clearer picture of what people really care about.

CASE STUDY Langley, Washington

That's exactly what happened in a series of public forums that were sparked last year in my hometown of Langley, Washington, over a developer's application to build a controversial new subdivision on the edge of town. The first session consisted mostly of the airing of opinions—many of them sharp but uninformed—and very little reflection. Responding to this meeting, the city council rejected the developer's application out of hand. When this action caused the developer to threaten to sue for failure to observe due process, the citizens took a deep breath and went back to the drawing board. In subsequent forums they went deeper than opinions and discovered that the challenge was not this one application but the whole long-range future of the town. They organized a community visioning process, which still continues, and are working with the city government to come up with a long-term land-use plan that meets the perceived needs that emerged from the forums. A much-scaled-down version of that original development has now been proposed that is in keeping with the emerging public will.

WHAT'S YOUR EXPERIENCE? ■ *Have you ever been part of a public meeting that went beyond opinions; that went deeper than arguments and positions? If you have, what was the result? How did you feel about that process?*

■ Support the Emerging Public Will with a Community Vision

Use the visioning process described in "What's the Vision for Your Project?" in chapter 2 as part of developing the public will behind an issue. It's a good way to help the community see what it can do and to get a more complete sense of community resources. When people create a community vision, they see possibilities for working together that they didn't see before. That can result in a new imagining of what might be, and a new and stronger motivation for action. That was certainly the case with Langley, in the example just above. It also happened in a neighboring town:

CASE STUDY Clinton, Washington

When the residents of this small town asked me for help in deciding how their town might grow, the challenge was daunting. Clinton is a ferry landing, and congestion on the only road up from the ferry splits the town in two every half hour, making any kind of community design difficult. A visioning process at a community forum proved to be a great tool for getting residents to "think outside the box" to identify their needs, preferences, and resources. Within an hour, they'd come up with several imaginative community designs that used the ferry dock as an asset and not an obstacle.

As the dialogue deepened, however, they also discovered that the public will in Clinton was for very modest growth—an outcome that was not evident when the forum started.

■ The Public Will Does Not Have to Be Unanimous

What you want is enough common ground to support political actions that all can live with. More than one action might be generated, but if the public will is strong enough and clear enough, multiple actions will be mutually reinforcing, or at least compatible.

■ Transform the Public Will into Public Action

As the public will begins to coalesce behind an issue, the task for the community then is to focus on action steps to implement that will. *What specifically needs to be done, by whom, and by when?* Now's the time to form a team (chapter 4) and create an action plan (chapter 5). In the Clinton example just above, once it was clear that the public will was for only modest growth, citizens then organized a group to oppose the creation of a municipal sewer system that might have doubled the size of the town.

WORKING WITH "THE SYSTEM"

This section refers mostly to institutions of government (at any level). The advice here, however, applies to dealing with *any*

Bill Levitt

Mayor Bill Levitt, of Alta, Utah, thinks his job description includes ensuring the well-being of his town, its 400 citizens, and all those who will treasure its stunning setting in generations to come. His efforts have brought him threats, lawsuits—and reelection nine times.

The job hasn't been easy and it hasn't been lucrative; Levitt's salary is a dollar a year. But when New Yorker Levitt first saw Alta back in 1954, he fell in love with its beauty and its people, and he settled in for the long haul, committed to preserving its wonders.

A former mining town, Alta gets 500 inches of good powder a year on its Wasatch Range slopes, so in the 1960s and '70s, when developers began moving into ski country, Alta—along with Vail, Aspen, and Snowmass—was a prime target for big changes.

Citizen, then Mayor, Levitt saw those changes bringing environmental degradation, soaring housing costs, and minimum-wage jobs, as other ski towns built jet-landing strips, luxury shopping malls, restaurants, condos, and mansions. It hasn't happened in Alta.

When developers apply for building permits, they get the news from City Hall that the town has no water rights or sewage hookups available. That's when the lawsuits get filed. And that's when threats institution, including corporations and large nonprofits, such as universities and hospitals.

■ Keep a Positive Attitude

Institutions often do not immediately respond to the public will. If they did, there would be no need for much of this book. In fact, it's easy to be negative about institutions because there's not one of us who hasn't had a miserable experience—or 8 or 10—in dealing with them. But stereotypes create self-fulfilling prophecies. If you really believe that "you can't fight city hall," then you probably can't. And if you really believe that institutions are myopic, impersonal, resistant forces whose faults can only be addressed with a sharp stick in the eye, then that's probably what it will take from you.

I'm not suggesting that you ignore the failings of the institutions you have to deal with. But I *am* suggesting that you keep sufficient faith in them and the bureaucratic systems they create and support. Remember that all institutions evolved as a way to provide more efficient delivery of goods or services, and that government institutions were created to promote uniform application of laws and regulations and to prevent arbitrary abuses of power. It's not easy to design institutions that will be fair and accessible to everyone, to maintain quality in them over the long term, and to put people in charge who will do the right thing most of the time. Sometimes I think it's a wonder the System works as well as it does.

have come in on Levitt's phone.

Alta does encourage development—of hiking trails. Some visitors are particularly welcome, like the geology students who come in from all over the world to study Alta's pristine ecological systems. And you can get a run on those deep powder slopes, but only five tour buses are allowed into the valley each day. Once in, you're guaranteed a beautiful, uncrowded run; if there are too many people on the slopes, the lifts are slowed down.

Mayor Levitt's vigilance affects people beyond those in the valley: 20 percent of the Salt Lake Valley's drinking water comes from this watershed that could be endangered by Aspen-style development.

Levitt says he's not antidevelopment, just deeply opposed to exploitation, and he walks his talk. His own land holdings are now the property of the U.S. Forest Service.

Now that he's passed 80, Bill Levitt is looking for a successor. Treasuring the quality of life their mayor has preserved, the citizens of Alta seem in no hurry to let him retire.

Tie every complaint to some constructive suggestion or action that might make the institution that's just failed you work better next time. Support reforms that will make institutions fairer and more responsive. Losing faith in institutions will ultimately make your work as an active citizen much harder because you will miss the many opportunities for working *with* them.

Ohio activist Evelyn Schaeffer puts it this way: "I don't think any-one can become a citizen activist if he or she doesn't, deep down, believe in the systems we develop to make our society function. Remember the original idea: good people who care about service in the public sector are making themselves available." See sidebar, page 164 for the story of Giraffe Bill Levitt, the mayor of Alta, Utah.

Suzanne Sinclair, auditor of Island County, Washington, adds this thought: "I don't always agree with what people are doing, but there aren't very many that are deliberately trying to make other people miserable. That goes for elected officials too. We don't always agree on any specific decision, but everyone I've met is trying to do what they think is the right thing. I get tired of the constant derision of elected representatives and officials, even though it's not generally aimed at me personally. It certainly makes one pause occasionally and reconsider exactly why it was that we decided to do this."

I agree with Schaeffer and Sinclair. It's tough to be in public office when uninformed people exercising their free speech call you names and blame you for things you may have no control over or responsi-bility for.

■ Connect with People—Get to "We"

What drives people crazy about institutions is often the bureau-cracies they develop to do their work, and the culture of inertia and buck passing that these bureaucracies often spawn. Bad bureaucra-cies are famously "faceless" because they lessen or even remove individual responsibility for results. If you're a bureaucrat in an institution, the more people you're surrounded by, the easier it becomes to hide an error, blame somebody else, or shrug your shoulders and forget about it. Another way to duck responsibility in a bureaucracy is to over-focus on process: doing things "right" becomes more important than doing the right thing, as when entering the data correctly into the system becomes more important than the integrity of the data.

TRY THIS ■ *The best way I've ever found to promote responsible behavior in a bureaucracy (fast results, good service, honest answers, and so on) is* to treat people in it as individuals—*in an environment in which they are too often treated like cogs in a machine.*

Treat people in bureaucracies with compassion and respect, and you'll be amazed by how well they respond. As a State Department officer, I met with hundreds of people. My attitude toward them got a lot more helpful when they treated me as a person—not just as some lever they were trying to pull in the State Department. And I closed down very quickly to anyone who assumed that I was the enemy or some dull bureaucrat without a brain or conscience.

Most people in bureaucracies are decent people trying to do the right thing in often difficult environments and, almost always, with impossible workloads. When I walk up to the counter in some massive gray public building these days, I think of those highway signs: "Road Crew Ahead—Give 'Em a Brake." Maybe it's because I know from experience how hard it can be to keep a positive spirit and do a good job inside a bureaucracy. Here's a story:

CASE STUDY The Manhattan DMV

I'm at the office of the Department of Motor Vehicles in Manhattan—about as impersonal, unhelpful, and unreasonable a bureaucracy as you can imagine. After an hour's wait in line, I finally step up to the window. What I need is New York plates to replace expired South Carolina ones on the 16-year-old Pontiac my wife's dad has just given us. I hand the 16-year-old South Carolina title papers to the clerk, who then goes to a massive volume of title forms and returns to tell me that the car can't be registered: the book has only 15 years' worth of forms for South Carolina, so according to the rules she can't tell for sure that my title is not a forgery.

She's about to yell "Next," and I'm about to explode. But I take a deep breath. In front of me, at least for the moment, I see not an unhelpful bureaucrat but a woman who's been on her feet forever, taking guff from an endless stream of demanding New Yorkers. What a job! And ahead of her there's probably a long subway trek home, cooking for her family, cleaning up, and dropping into a chair too tired to read the paper. Does she want to be an unhelpful bureaucrat? Who would, really? Would she appreciate being treated like a real human being? Of course. Does she have a sense of humor? I decide to find out.

I take the car keys for that Pontiac out of my pocket and slide them across the counter to her. "You want a car?" I say. "It's got a couple of rust spots, but it runs fine." She stares at me, uncertain. Then I say—with a smile—"Well, without valid plates, I can't drive it out of the parking lot, right?" Then I add, "I think we have a problem here."

The most important word I said was "we." That one word communicated to that clerk that I was talking to her as somebody with a brain and a heart, asking her to treat me the same way. She didn't contest my use of "we" because she saw, perhaps better than I did, the idiocy in the rigid regs that she was paid to enforce. Now here was what seemed to be a nice guy in front of her, asking for her help. It was a chance for her to bust out of the DMV cog-ness and to actually use her head and her heart to be of service. I doubt that she actually thought it all through that way, but she ended up looking at me for a few seconds and then breaking up laughing. Then she started conspiring with me to get around the rule. I left with plates, and she headed for the subway that night knowing that she was one public servant that day who had been human, resourceful, and truly of service.

What I did was no big deal—just checking my anger enough to see the humanity in an overworked clerk, and taking a chance that something good might happen. I certainly had nothing to lose by trying.

I call this approach "Getting to We," and it works just about every time. I think that's so because most people—at least those who are not completely soul-dead—want and need to do things with their lives that they see as meaningful. It's tough to find a lot of meaning in bureaucratic work. So when the opportunity is presented to people in a bureaucracy to take initiative, exercise some caring, *and* solve a problem all at the same time, for many of them the motivation to do so is strong.

Finally, remember the Emergency Room Syndrome: to the doctor on call it's the 100th broken arm he's seen this month, but for me it's *my* broken arm and it hurts like hell. To the bureaucrat or official who's responsible for handling hundreds of problems, *my* problems may not be particularly unique or compelling. It's fair for you to be relentless in pushing and prodding things along, but it may not be fair to come unglued because it isn't going as fast as you'd like.

■ Learn to Dance with the Elephant

No matter how helpful individual bureaucrats might be, the very size and nature of bureaucracy can create frustrating problems for activists. One of those problems is finding where the decision makers are who can make the changes you want. Buck passing is a big temptation in institutions, so finding the right person can be difficult. In environmental work, for example, there's often a complex interplay between federal, state, and local laws. There's no point in focusing your resources on the local county council if, in fact, it's the state legislature that controls the issue that concerns you.

KEY POINT ■ *Focus on the right part of the right institution or you'll end up chasing your own tail.*

Another challenge for the activist is compartmentalization—the tendency of bureaucracies to put the various things you need done into so many different pigeonholes that it becomes very hard for you, or even for the people who work there, to see how all the tasks relate, let alone how to get them all done. Dealing with this can be like trying to conduct a symphony without a score.

TRY THIS ■ *Before you start, acquaint yourself with the institution's wiring diagram so that you can better see the path to a decision. Then create a coordinated campaign that allows you to progress through the maze without losing sight of where you ultimately want to end up, and without being defeated by a runaround.*

A third way in which large bureaucracies can defeat activists is through sheer volume—submerging you with documents, hearings, and procedures, and sucking you into a legal and bureaucratic morass from which they may hope you never emerge.

In my experience, however, citizen activists can play this game much better than even the largest bureaucracy, for the simple reason that citizens are volunteers. While the bureaucracy must pay staff and consultants to submerge you in paper, you have far fewer billable hours—maybe none at all. The Citizens' Coalition in Island County, for example, assembled a team of more than 20 people who researched and wrote position papers on every aspect of the county's planning. Our papers were as good as or better than anything the county's high-priced contractors could write. In the end, we overwhelmed *them* with ideas and options rather than the other way around.

Finally, every institution develops its own jargon, and half the time people in it don't even realize that they use jargon, technical terms, or acronyms that mean nothing to outsiders or, worse, leave them uninformed or misled.

TRY THIS ■ *Learn the lingo. It's fine to poke fun at the way bureaucrats can massacre the language, but it's also important that you learn enough of the in-house speech that you don't miss or misunderstand important communications.*

■ In Unity There Is Strength

The more ambitious your effort to effect change, the more necessary it becomes to recruit allies. But the bigger your coalition

Carl Ross believes that grass-roots activism can change the world, and he's dedicating his life to that belief. As cofounder of Save America's Forests (SAF), a nonprofit lobbying group, Ross lobbies daily against forces that want to cut old-growth forests. His record is solid. Through unrelenting lobbying and educating of politicians, tiny SAF has repeatedly attracted strong congressional support for forest-protection bills.

Ross and two others started SAF in 1990 as a national network to enlist all environmental groups in a coalition to press for legislation that would save America's trees. It hasn't worked out that smoothly. Ross works to rally environmental groups behind the bills in question, but some of the larger and better-known groups have seen SAF's less compromising approach as undermining their efforts. Ross has also been attacked in the press as too extreme.

In spite of all these difficulties, Ross is undaunted. His viewpoint is that SAF has sparked needed energy and built the overall effectiveness of environmental lobbying: "We got the environmental movement out of the doldrums," he says.

Lobbying politicians and rallying grassroots environmental groups are only parts of SAF's work. Another major thread is training the next generation of becomes, the harder it is to maintain its cohesion and consistency. Institutions are perfectly capable of trying to take advantage of this by singling out parts of your coalition for special treatment. This usually takes the form of offering special deals to one faction in the hopes of pulling it out of the coalition and weakening the joint effort. A nastier form of this kind of gamesmanship is to badmouth one or several leaders of the change effort in the hopes of undermining the group's trust in its own leadership.

The best inoculation against divide-and-conquer tactics is impeccable communications within your group, mutual trust you've cultivated from the get-go, and a strong, shared team vision of the results you want. If efforts are made to pull your team apart, these elements will give it the strength to stay unified.

LOBBYING

Special thanks for many of the tips in this section to Samuel Halperin and the American Youth Policy Forum, 1836 Jefferson Place, NW, Washington, D.C. 20036.

Lobbying is trying to persuade a government decision maker to cast a vote or take an action that you favor. It can be done in person or by letter, fax, or e-mail. Although most lobbying is done by professional firms, amateurs with a persuasive case can often have more of an influence in decision makers' offices than paid lobbyists, whose faces and views are all too well known (see Giraffe Carl Ross's story on page 170).

A GIRAFFE STORY
continued

environmental activists. SAF regularly has 10 to 12 interns learning environmental law and the political process. Many of them go on to careers in places such as the Natural Resources Division of the Justice Department.

SAF also provides citizen education. Its Web site offers a Citizen Action Guide full of information about upcoming forest legislation and existing laws, the effects of clear-cutting, and the status of endangered species.

Ross is sure that environmental protection will someday be the norm in our culture rather than a matter of ongoing dispute. "It took hundreds of years to end slavery and to secure women's right to vote," says Carl Ross, who led his first save-the-trees campaign at age 19, rallying neighbors in Plainview, New York. "Forest protection is doing amazingly well for a movement that's only decades old."

Look for Ross to be hanging in for the long haul, working for that day when there are no more disputes about environmental protection.

Web link: Save America's Forests (www.saveamericasforests.org).

Never underestimate the power of contacting your elected or appointed officials. In the distant past I worked as an aide to Senator John Glenn. While the senator certainly didn't ignore piles of form letters from large lobbying groups or visits from lobbyists for powerful commercial interests, time after time I saw him pay attention to a few well-directed messages or visits from nonprofessionals—or even just one—if the point was clear and from the heart.

Here are tips on how to prepare and deliver a lobbying message, whether by mail, fax, e-mail, or in person:

■ *Know your issue—otherwise you'll just be wasting a busy person's time.*

■ *If writing, faxing, or e-mailing, address your messages accurately. Addresses of public officials are a matter of public record. Find them on the Web or in print directories (see "Resources").*

■ *If writing, faxing, or e-mailing about more than one issue, send a separate message for each one. If your message contains multiple subjects, there's a good chance that copies will not be made or sent and that your message will go into only one folder and not any others.*

■ *Find out what you can about the people you will be lobbying. The more you know about policy makers and their interests, committee assignments, and so on, the better able you'll be to plan your approach and the more likely you'll be to establish rapport with them. For national and statewide offices, consult Michael Barone's* The Almanac of American Politics, *the U.S. Congressional Directory or its state equivalent, or the Internet. For local offices, ask people who know the official you want to contact.*

■ *Clearly identify the bill or issue you're concerned about, either by number or by a popular title. Policy makers must deal with many issues, so it's important to be specific.*

■ *Be timely. Your communication has to get to policy makers well before the decisions must be made.*

■ *Be reasonably brief and very clear about the results you want. Whether in print or in person, you may have only a few minutes of the policy maker's attention—don't waste it with generalities.*

■ *Make your case. Don't just urge a vote in a particular direction. Give the reasons for your position and show why it is the best course. Back up your arguments with enough pertinent facts and figures without burying the policy maker in statistics. Provide additional details as attachments and leave-behinds, including any supportive media articles you may have. Policy makers cannot possibly have ready access to expertise in all the fields they have to address, and they usually welcome information and advice from constituents who have relevant knowledge.*

- *Acknowledge the policy maker's interests. Show specifically how doing what you want done will be to his or her benefit.*

- *Be respectful in dress and attitude. If lobbying in person, don't let your appearance distract from your message. Dress conservatively. Never berate or threaten policy makers—don't give them an excuse for dismissing you and your cause.*

- *Be as positive as possible. Begin your letter or visit by congratulating the policy maker for something she or he has done right (even if you have to dig for it). Officials are human, too; they appreciate an occasional "Well done" and will reward it with more attention to the next point you want to make.*

- *Use your own words; don't simply parrot somebody else's. Policy makers already know what the major lobbying groups are saying, but they don't know of your experiences and observations, or what the proposed bill or policy or action will do to you and for you personally. Sending form letters and form e-mails is usually not worth the trouble. The only time I do it is if some well-organized mass effort aims to deliver them by the millions. Then they are noticed. Not read, but noticed.*

- *If lobbying in person with a group, agree on a common approach before the meeting, appoint a lead spokesperson, and don't squabble in front of the person you're trying to influence. If your group doesn't have its own act together, you can't expect a policy maker to be persuaded.*

- *Don't make promises you can't keep or pretend to wield influence you don't have. Policy makers have staffs, and if they're interested enough, they can do research on you. If they conclude that you're a blusterer, you can kiss good-bye your chances of influencing their decisions.*

- *If you're lobbying in person, summarize the main points of your discussion before you leave, and press for specific agreements on commitments and follow-up actions. A good question to ask on parting is "What else would you like me to do to follow up on this issue, and when?" Thank the policy maker for his or her time and concern. The next day, send a thank-you note that briefly reiterates your concern and accurately notes whatever agreements were reached.*

- Maintain the relationships. Don't overwhelm policy makers with visits or communications, but do stay in touch. Invite them to events and to tours of your work so that they can get a better hands-on feel for what you're doing.

- Lobby through the newspapers. Elected officials always read the letters to the editor in the hometown papers, which provides another incentive for your group to place a steady stream of them (see "Letters to the Editor, Op-Eds, and Talk Shows" in chapter 9, page 154).

PLAY IT AGAIN

> **WHAT'S NEXT?**
> The next chapter looks at two more ways to solve public problems: public testimony and legal action.

- Develop the public will. If you've got it behind you and your cause, it becomes an important source of leverage:

  - Use public forums to develop the public will.

  - Developing the public will requires going deeper than just asking for opinions.

  - Support the emerging public will with a community vision—then transform public will into public action.

- Learn how to work successfully with "the System":

  - Keep a positive attitude.

  - Treat people in bureaucracies as individuals, in an environment in which they are too often treated like cogs in a machine.

  - Focus on the right part of the right institution or you'll end up chasing your own tail.

  - Build relationships within your team. It's the best way to defeat the divide-and-conquer tactics that institutions can sometimes use against you.

- Lobby decision makers to cast votes or take actions that you favor:

  - Know your issue and find out what you can about the person you'll be lobbying.

  - Be reasonably brief—and very clear—about the results you want. Give your reasons for taking a stand and back them up. Acknowledge the policy maker's interests, too.

  - Be timely. Your communication has to get to policy makers well before the decisions must be made.

  - Be respectful in tones and words, and as positive as possible.

  - Communicate your own views, or at least don't simply parrot somebody else's.

- If lobbying in person with a group, agree on a common approach before the meeting and appoint a lead spokesperson.

- Don't make promises you can't keep or pretend to wield influence you don't have.

- If lobbying in person, summarize the main points of your discussion before you leave, and press for specific agreements on commitments and follow-up actions.

- Maintain the relationships you form.

- Lobby through the newspapers. Elected officials always read the letters to the editor in the hometown papers.

*People can be divided into three groups: those who make
things happen, those who watch things happen, and those
who wonder what happened.*
NICHOLAS MURRAY BUTLER

■

PUBLIC TESTIMONY AND LEGAL ACTION

HEARING ROOMS and courtrooms are important arenas for citizen activists. You need to know how to act in them.

PUBLIC TESTIMONY

Most government institutions are committed by law or practice to give citizens an organized way to make their voices heard, usually through some form of public meeting or hearing. Often hearings are a mandated part of any process involving major expenditures of public funds, or major changes in public policy or provision of basic services—from building a new sports stadium to changing zoning rules. Even if a hearing on your issue is mandated, however, you may have to push to have one in your area. The opportunities and rules will be different in each locale.

Here are steps for making your participation at a hearing as effective as possible:

■ Prepare Well

Know the ground rules. Make sure you know the *form* the hearing will take. Hearings before legislative bodies, for example, are *legislative hearings*, and the point is to influence laws, policies, and/or the appropriation of funds by describing your experience and delivering your point of view. Hearings before regulatory commissions are often *quasi-judicial*, which means they are much like courts of law, in which the party against whom the complaint has been brought is treated as the defendant. Because of this, quasi-judicial hearings are usually more formal than legislative hearings.

KEY POINT ■ *Don't count on anyone telling you the rules of the game in advance.*

It's up to you to find out what kind of hearing you are heading for, and the rules and procedures in effect. When and how long will you be allowed to speak, for example? Will there be give and take, and if so, what procedures apply to that? If it's a quasi-judicial hearing, will you be expected to call witnesses?

Understand the issues and the people. Review the guidance on doing research (see "Research" in chapter 2, page 17). You'll do yourself more harm than good if you show up at a public hearing unprepared, simply mouthing a complaint without substantiating your case. Judges and commissioners listen to complaints all day long, and their eyes glaze over. What you need to give them is a well-researched and cohesive argument, buttressed with persuasive anecdotes. The overall picture you want to present is that your group is committed, knows the issue well, and won't be satisfied with sops or dismissed with nonanswers and runarounds.

Find out as much as you can in advance about the other people who will be at the hearing, especially those who might be testifying against your position and the policy makers who will hear the testimony. Try to put yourself in the shoes of those policy makers—to see the issues and the hearing as they see them. Given their concerns, politics, and points of view, what can you say that will be most convincing to them? Beyond making your case and thanking them for their attention, think about what elements of their self-interests you might (discreetly) touch on—for example, what are the political advantages to them of following your lead?

Follow the money. It's amazing how much clearer issues become when you track down who makes money from a government or corporate decision. I'm not talking about corruption—just who will profit. Road-paving firms profit from more and wider roads; builders profit from looser building codes; real estate brokers profit from subsidized housing programs, and so on. A little time spent following the money trail will help you spot allies and opponents in the room.

Make a plan. Decide in advance what your team's overall testimony needs to achieve, and then divide up the work in your group. Cover all the bases, including technical comments, economic impacts, environmental assessments, transportation impacts, and legal ramifications. Assemble key data in handouts that convey the essence of your message. Then weave the testimony from all of your team's speakers into a cohesive plan. Choose as your wrap-up speaker someone who can think fast and can summarize opposing views and answer them. For tips on organizing teams, see chapter 4. For advice on delivering a public presentation, see chapter 8.

Fill the room. Packing the room with people who share your point of view has an impact on decision makers, no matter how much they may say it doesn't. A recent hearing before our county commission about plans for a large resort is an excellent example. Many expected this hearing to be a slam-dunk approval. But well-organized and well-prepared anti-resort activists packed the room. Their excellent testimony was persuasive, but so too were the hundreds of pairs of eyes looking straight at the commissioners for two hours, the sentiments behind them undisguised.

TRY THIS ■ *No matter how many people you have at a hearing, the official transcript will show just the names of those people who actually testified during the day—which may be only 20 to 30. So prepare your own sign-in sheet and make sure that everyone who comes, even for a few minutes, signs it. Then submit it as part of the record at the end of the day.*

Dress appropriately. Respect your audience in your tone, style, and dress. If any one of these things is too different from what the people in the audience are comfortable with, it can and probably will keep them from hearing what you say. If you have doubts about what's appropriate, ask someone who's been there, or go to a hearing and observe.

I know a very smart environmental activist who refuses to clean up before he speaks at government hearings; to him, it's a matter of principle. Fine, that's his right. But I don't have much patience when this same guy complains that the officials don't want to listen to him. The officials interpret his "style" as a lack of respect for them—and they're right.

Never assume that the decision makers have the facts they need. Hand out copies of your statement (or a crisp summary of it) and relevant supporting data to all the people you are testifying before (and to the media, if they are present) so that they can look at you instead of scribbling notes while you're talking. You might also list your key facts as bullet points on one piece of paper (or on a card) that can be distributed to everybody at the hearing, digested easily, and carried around in a briefcase or coat pocket.

CASE STUDY Ashtabula County, Ohio

Evelyn Schaeffer writes: "I knew that since this was a quasi-judicial process with the phone companies as defendants, they were probably going to sit tight and not volunteer any information, on attorneys' advice. So I prepared a complete set of overheads showing each area where calling essential services meant making a long distance call. I gave the chairman of the Public Utilities Commission (PUCO) a copy of my facts and he used it as reference throughout the day. I did this with the attitude of 'You just must not have all this information, because if you did you would see the problem and it would have been fixed long ago.' Much later I found out the extent to which PUCO did not have even the most basic facts about phone service in rural areas."

■ Be as Engaging, Personal, and Positive as You Can Be

Avoid simply reading a statement, if you can, especially if you've already handed it out. Don't be afraid to extemporize—you want to express your convictions in a clear, engaging, and authoritative way. If something's been said by somebody else that significantly contradicts or supports what you intend to say, show the policy makers that you're alert by referring to it in an appropriate way. Reread chapter 8, on persuasive communications.

Tell your own story. Policy makers by and large *want* to help people, and they respond to personal anecdotes and stories by or about people who are directly affected by the issues.

<hr>

CASE STUDY Island County

Island County Commissioner Bill Thorn writes: "At a series of hearings on whether or not to ban County use of chemical sprays to control weeds on County roads, several people were quite militant and threatening about suing us if we continued to spray. There were also several technical anti-spray presentations that seemed to be based on data that I thought was questionable or biased. All this fell on deaf ears with my fellow Commissioners and to some extent with me. What turned the tide was a meeting one day with the courtroom packed with no-spray advocates. Three or four chemically sensitive people presented their personal stories of the trials of living with this condition. Between the large number of people in the room and the moving personal stories, I could see the minds of my two fellow Commissioners changing. We were all touched by the stories—and the spraying was banned."

<hr>

AVOID THIS MISTAKE ■ *Don't be so engaging that you ignore time limits, which might be as short as three minutes at a crowded hearing. If you know that testimonies will be closely timed, time your own statement beforehand to make sure you will not be cut off in mid-point. I often prepare long and short versions of what I want to say, as time limits can suddenly change.*

<hr>

Keep the tone positive. Anyone who has ever served on a local board will tell you how refreshing it is to hear a well-crafted presentation respectfully delivered. A positive tone encourages the room to listen to what you have to say, and it helps build the mutual respect that allows all sides to look for common ground. Using a positive tone most definitely does not mean being naive. You will always have to make tough-minded assessments and decisions, but you can do so without impugning others' motives, and with a vision of results that serve all sides.

CASE STUDY Ashtabula County, Ohio

Again, Evelyn Schaeffer writes:

> I asked everyone who testified from our group to speak positively about why eliminating local long distance calls was the right thing to do. The message was "Let's take this historic opportunity to fix this problem together: the public needs this; our local phone companies (of course) want to give their customers what they need; and the Public Utilities Commission (PUCO), as the overseeing body, wants to make that happen." The hearing was standing room only, and by about 4 p.m. the look on the face of the PUCO chairman was priceless as yet another copy of testimony was dropped on the pile in front of him. The look on the faces of the execs of the phone companies and their lawyer was pretty good too; they didn't know what to do with no antagonism and confrontation in the room.

> We kept relentlessly pursuing our strategy of "You the phone company are part of our community and we know you are good corporate citizens and want to do what's best." It's clear that by approaching the first hearing in this way, we got both the companies' and PUCO's attention in a positive way and built trust with both that we were not a bunch of hotheads . . .

> As we persisted in our quest over the next several years, it was this foundation that kept our lines of communication open, both with the phone companies and with PUCO.

Be more open than you're comfortable with being. You've read my story in chapter 7 about the value of being open with officials in

Island County (page 108). Here's Evelyn Schaeffer's assessment of the same approach:

Island County (page 108).

CASE STUDY Ashtabula County, Ohio

"One principle I started out with and always followed," Evelyn Schaeffer writes, "was to always communicate what we were doing to the 'opposition.' That sure kept the lines of communication open with the phone companies . . . their attorneys couldn't ever believe that they really did already know everything I had up my sleeve. I think that may be part of what caused the president of the company to break precedent, ignore the standard legal defense against 'consumer demands,' and look for a real solution. He knew we weren't going away because he always knew what we were doing."

KEY POINT ■ *Openness in the public process, especially when everyone else is playing their cards close to the vest, can often dramatically shift the energy in a room, prompting the kind of mutual honesty that builds trust and leads to common ground.*

Of course there are limits on when and how open you can be. It may be clear from your opponents' responses, for example, that they, or the people before whom you're testifying, are determined not to walk through the door you've opened. If they simply try to take advantage of your candor, then you've got little choice but to put up your own armor.

My experience, however, is that most activists err on the other side—they are too cautious about being open, especially in public negotiations and testimony. Openness is a risk, but the benefits can be enormous and the risk is usually well worth taking.

■ Don't Overreach

Some issues you may deal with are large, complex, and represented by powerful constituencies on both sides. In such cases, it's often not possible to get everything you want in one campaign—the political power, public opinion, or legal precedents you need may simply not be there. If it becomes clear that this is the case, the best course is to proceed incrementally. With the Island County Citizens' Coalition, for example, after four years of work we had reached 80 percent of our initial goals. We left 20 percent for the next round, not because we were exhausted, but because we understood that we had pushed county leaders—and many of the people in the county—about as far as we could at that time without destroying the respectful and productive relationships we had built with both.

CASE STUDY Island County

Island County Commissioner Bill Thorn relates this story about another group that took another tack: "I very clearly remember one hearing late in the process," Thorn writes, "where we wanted to wrap up the final disagreements in a dispute on habitat preservation. The group pressing us to take an extreme position came in with a surly attitude and presented their case. The Commissioners were prepared to give them 75 percent of what they were asking and we said so. The group caucused for a brief time and came back as if they had not heard a thing we offered. Not only did they not acknowledge the County's offer, they withdrew every concession they'd made previously. The Commissioners were completely turned off by this tactic and the hearing ended badly. We ended up in court. It took two years to sort out the issue there, ending up—after considerable trouble and expense—very close to what this group could have gotten in the first place if they had not overreached."

LEGAL ACTION

As citizens today, we've got many tools to promote political and social change. We can bring to bear the focused power of the public will, using forums, media, hearings, and public education. We can lobby and negotiate. We can vote leaders in and out of office. We can help move bureaucracies to function as they're supposed to.

But there are times when that's not enough. There are times when the powers opposing you are just too entrenched and impermeable. And from the school board that's lousing up your kid's education to the government that's caving in to special interests, institutions can sometimes seem faceless, mindless, and as hard to turn as an aircraft carrier.

Unless you want to give up, you have to move to more confrontational methods. Chief among these is legal action. One advantage of seeking what you want in the courts is the possibility of gaining justice that you might not get otherwise. The courts are a vital means of protecting constitutional rights and enforcing laws and regulations passed to protect the public good. Without the power of the courts to enforce environmental laws in the United States, for example, most polluting industries wouldn't bother to comply.

Another benefit, from my experience, is that legal action, and threats of legal action, can be very useful as a means of getting the attention of an institution that doesn't want to change, and of convincing it of the strength and determination of the forces pushing against it.

CASE STUDY Island County

When Washington State passed its Growth Management Act (GMA), Island County's three commissioners chose to ignore the law because it would force them to implement restrictions on property rights and land use that they (and their core constituencies) strongly opposed. When we formed the Citizens' Coalition to push for implementation of the GMA, we were essentially ignored by these commissioners—until we made it clear that we were prepared to go to court to enforce compliance. From that point on, we were able to accomplish a great deal through negotiations and testimony, and eventually we forged considerable common ground by slowly building trust and respect with these commissioners and with our other political opponents. Still, there is no doubt that litigation, and threats of litigation, were major factors in getting people to listen to us.

In Island County it was the citizens that initiated legal action. But sometimes you might be forced into court because your adversaries have filed suit to get what *they* want, and you have no choice but to meet them on that field. Your adversaries might sue, for example, to gain a variance in a statute, a change in a zoning code, an exemption from a requirement, or the dismissal of a complaint. Well-funded corporations under fire from citizen activists also sometimes file knowingly frivolous suits against activists for the sole purpose of intimidation.

KEY POINT ■ *Whether or not you initiate the action, it's important to understand how the legal system works and how to work within it.*

■ Legal Action—the Dangers

Legal action can be a valuable tool in the public process, but there are plenty of downsides as well. Legal action should be used sparingly, and only after much reflection and preparation. Here's why I urge so much caution:

You could lose. Legal losses tend to be long-term and expensive.

Legal action is conflict. In today's courtrooms, legal proceedings are almost always confrontational—they pit people against each other. While some lawyers and some courts may try to find common ground between opposing parties, the legal system as a whole is far more likely to create winners and losers.

As we all know, conflict impedes honest communication and stirs emotions, which makes compromise difficult to impossible as egos and tempers flare.

The rancor created in most courtrooms also undermines opportunities for long-term solutions. Rancor makes it far more difficult, for example, for the parties involved to even consider trusting each other after a court-ordered settlement, let alone continue to work for long-term solutions that reflect a genuine commonality of interests.

A good current example is the Endangered Species Act. It has been the subject of bitter court fights for more than three decades, and there is virtually no honest dialogue left in a situation that has become totally polarized between those who want to gut the act and those who will not permit even the smallest tweaks.

Without making a joke about it, a big part of this problem is lawyers. Lawyers are trained to be antagonists, not peacemakers. Although some of my lawyer friends say this may be changing, most lawyers still see their primary function as doing battle. They get good at fighting, not at resolving fights. A rationale is that clients are to be "protected" from the ugliness and complexity of conflict.

I can still remember one awful afternoon when my first wife and I met, each with our lawyer, to settle issues in our divorce. We had privately settled most of the issues already and had done so more or less civilly. Once in the room with lawyers, however, we were both told to keep quiet, and the two lawyers started going at each other like junkyard dogs. My wife and I looked at each other in disbelief. Then we pulled the lawyers off, and told them to shut up and simply draw up papers to reflect what we both thought was fair.

Your lawsuit may create enemies outside the courtroom. Not everybody may be thrilled with what you are trying to do, and the criticisms and counteractions could be harsh. Giraffe Jerry Bilinski had to take on people in his own community in his fight for at-risk kids (see sidebar on this page).

Legal action lets everyone duck responsibilities they should be facing. Once a disputed matter gets into the courts, it's just too easy for both sides to hide behind their lawyers, avoiding the risk and trouble of trying to find true solutions built on common ground.

In court, too many people cede their power to lawyers and accept conflict rather than take the risks and do the hard work of caring and reconciliation. It's much easier to turn it all over to the attorney and do whatever he or she says. If you

A GIRAFFE STORY
Jerry Bilinski

Jerry Bilinski knows that life can be unfair. He's been working for decades with kids who've been abused, neglected, and shuffled through the New York City foster-care system. But there's a limit to what he can stand. It was way too much when community pressure threatened to close a Patchogue, New York, group home for disadvantaged teenagers where Bilinski was the resident houseparent.

There had been resistance to the foster home by some village residents in the 1970s. The black and Latino young men at the home were often singled out for disapproval in the predominantly white community.

The agency that sponsored the house caved in to the community's demands and, in the fall of 1993, ordered the group home closed. So Bilinski went into action: on his own, he filed a federal lawsuit and a fair-housing complaint with the U.S. Department of Housing and Urban Development. Among the defendants named in the lawsuit were Patchogue's mayor and its chamber of commerce president.

"I had to do something about what the community was doing," Bilinski says. "By forcing this home to close, it was stigmatizing every kid in it." As the boys' sole defender, Bilinski was ostracized by neighbors, harassed by police, and verbally attacked at public do that, it becomes much more difficult to build the relationships that might save the situation, because your lawyer will tell you to communicate with the other side only through him or her. What a relief! All you have to do is say, "I can't comment on advice of counsel." And none of this wussy stuff about developing a trusting relationship with your opponent!

■ How to Use Legal Action

A good threat can be almost as powerful as the real thing. The Citizens' Coalition in Island County was never secretive about its willingness to go to court. We made that threat credible, first, by raising enough money to file suits and making sure our opponents knew that, and second, by making good on the threat in the several instances when we were pushed to that point. Giraffe Ray Proffitt uses the same strategy (see sidebar, page 190).

Hire the right lawyer. Legal action often requires specialized legal assistance, for example in corporate, consumer, or environmental law. A local attorney who does not specialize in the field in which you're taking legal action isn't much better off than a well-briefed citizen activist. Interview prospective attorneys carefully with this in mind. And don't assume that the best in the field is beyond your price range. It's not uncommon for attorneys to lower their fees, sometimes dramatically, to take on issues they care about. It never hurts to ask.

Don't wait too long to seek legal help. If it appears that legal action is likely (or possible), at least consult with a lawyer as early in the

A GIRAFFE STORY
continued

meetings, in letters to the newspapers, and in anonymous telephone calls and mail. Hardest for him to take was getting no backing from his employers, who wanted Bilinski to drop the lawsuit. When he refused, he was forced to resign and spent the next eight months out of work.

Bilinski put over a thousand hours into researching and filing the lawsuit on behalf of the kids. The $500 filing fee came out of his own pocket, and he kept his promise to keep the house open as long as possible.

He managed to keep the house open until the boys finished their school year, and he got the town of Patchogue to establish a college scholarship fund for the kids and to publish a public statement of commitment to fair housing.

Jerry Bilinski is now working for Boys' Hope, a Staten Island organization that helps boys without money get to college. Looking back at Patchogue, Bilinski says, "There comes a time when you've just got to stand up and say, 'That's wrong.'"

process as you can. "I can't tell you," writes environmental lawyer Toby Thaler, "how many times I've seen neighborhood or grassroots activists come to the lawyer *after* the record is made or the issues framed and then ask us do-gooder lawyers to try to clean up the mess. Often, we will say 'too late' since by then the non-lawyer-advised record or issue-framing can't really be fixed."

Plan well. The legal system is high stakes and it is costly. You must understand clearly why you are going to court before you get there. What's your vision of success? What's your irreducible bottom line? Sit down with your attorney and discuss these issues. Have him outline the procedures for you, and the probable responses from your opponents. Get from him a sober assessment of the odds of your success, and its costs.

Then make a plan that is strong enough to guide your strategy but flexible enough to take advantage of fast-breaking events. If your legal actions are poorly planned or scattershot, decision makers will start to doubt your competence. Good planning also minimizes legal fees that would be wasted if you were constantly shifting strategies and tactics.

Your first legal steps are crucial—once you're in the legal system, everything you submit or say is on the record and can't be withdrawn. You need to get it right from the get-go.

Maintain control of your side's legal strategy. What you want from your attorney is advice, not take-it-or-leave-it orders.

Don't buy into the common perception of court proceedings as combat. In chapter 7, I pointed out the dangers and lost opportunities if a confrontational model for dealing with conflict is the *only* model you've got. Vanquished enemies will fight back the first chance they get. To the extent that you can move beyond confrontation into negotiation, however, the changes you seek will have staying power, and you at least open the possibility of achieving results better than what you could have possibly achieved through continued conflict.

You, your team, and your lawyer must all accept this basis for action, or no attempt at moving to negotiations can work. In particular, your lawyer's personality and reputation are important factors.

If seeking common ground is important to you, your lawyer must be able to earn respect, build trust, and negotiate creative solutions of mutual benefit.

AVOID THIS MISTAKE ■ *What you* don't *want in a lawyer is a junkyard dog that will terrorize the other side.*

Your lawyer's first message to the other side sets a tone that cannot easily be changed. Don't let him or her threaten. What's needed is a calm, professional message that lays out your interpretation of the legal issues.

KEY POINT ■ *Never burn your bridges behind you, because you never know what's coming next.*

A legal opponent in one battle may be someone you are courting as an ally in another. You and your attorney need to avoid cheap shots, attacks on character, and dishonest or underhanded moves. Such tactics may feel good, and may even result in fleeting advantages, but they create long-term baggage you don't want to carry around.

CASE STUDY Island County

If there was one thing it did very right in its legal actions in Island County, the Citizens' Coalition never lost sight of its long-term goals. We never let bridges burn to the point where they couldn't be crossed. We were constantly looking for opportunities to move from legal action back to negotiation (and twice did so, to good effect). We gained at least the grudging respect of most of our opponents and established some respectful alliances and collaborations that still exist.

Legal action should never be the only arrow in your quiver. At some point it's important to move the issues out of court and to establish working relationships with the people in the institutions your legal action is seeking to shift. If your opponents see that they will be sued no matter what they do, they have no incentive to cooperate, negotiate, or try in any other way to seek genuine common ground.

Your long-term goal should be more than a court order in your favor. As valuable as such an order may be, it's no substitute for long-term solutions that are stable, not because they rest on the decision of a judge or jury, but because they are the result of honest talk and patient efforts to build common ground. Never lose your own trust that there are decent people trying to do decent jobs on all sides of an issue— people who can summon the courage and compassion to act responsibly in tough situations, and who can see, or be helped to see, beyond short-term gain.

KEY POINT ■ *From the opening exchange of letters to the final arguments in court, never give up on the possibility of an out-of-court settlement.*

Often legal action will push both sides to an abyss; staring into that abyss can create incentives to try one more time to go back to the bargaining table and avoid the courtroom. Make sure you've kept the legal proceedings from descending into the kind of rancor that makes such reasonable reactions very difficult if not impossible.

Attorney Tim Martin, of Langley, Washington, offers this sound advice:

It is important to remember that any litigation may be settled at any time, regardless of the positions that have been established by the parties. No

---

Ray Proffitt

Ray Proffitt is known to some people as "the river vigilante," a man worth his weight in gold. To others he's a royal pain in the profit margin.

A former test pilot and stock-broker, Proffitt appointed himself protector of the Delaware River and its tributaries in the early 1990s. His flamboyant operations began with regular cruises along the waterways in a small plane or in an amphibious vehicle that looks like a car being driven into the river. Proffitt looked for any sign of trouble—the appearance of asphalt and concrete dumps in a marshland, untreated sewage outfall from a town, a new drainpipe pouring out industrial waste.

If he found pollution, he traced it to the source and confronted the offenders with his log notes and photographs. If they didn't stop polluting and clean up the messes they'd made, Proffitt took the offenders to court under the Clean Water Act.

Since those beginnings, Proffitt and the Ray Proffitt Foundation he started (RPF) have sued land developers, corporations, and towns on various environmental issues, including water quality, wetlands, solid waste, and mining. Usually RPF suits cause the accused to scramble into compliance with the law and avoid court: when a case does go to trial, offenders are often hit with heavy

---

matter how entrenched the opposition—or your own group—may appear, the possibility of a negotiated resolution should never be totally dismissed. More than once I have been involved in bitter, multi-year litigation, where settlement appeared virtually impossible, but, surprisingly, agreement was reached.

A common factor in each of those cases was the application of creativity: the ability to intellectually step back, take a fresh look at an old problem, and see a new way to reach common ground. In each of those cases, deep into the litigation process, someone suggested a new solution to a key issue, which, in turn, led to the resolution of other issues. Creative thinking should not end when litigation begins.

Take advantage of the delays that the legal system provides. Once you enter the legal arena, the action tends to slow way down as various court procedures are ordered and satisfied, and because court dockets are often crowded. Don't go to sleep during these delays. Stay in contact with the other side. New information or new events during a protracted delay may present fresh opportunities for a negotiated settlement.

■ And Beyond Legal Action?

The instinct for self-preservation in institutions is very strong. The more powerful that institutions become, the more they tend to protect their power and defend the status quo—which means that the odds are almost always stacked against those who want to change them. For much of world history, people who challenged institutions often had to resort to confrontations, which were sometimes violent. Here's a view from Toby Thaler, a Seattle lawyer: "In the big picture," Thaler writes, "those in control of institutions don't give a damn for the rest of us. . . . In the course of history and progress toward democracy and civil rights, most if not *all* major advances have been the result of nonnegotiated power shifts. People in the streets. People in courts. The English, French, and American revolutions were not negotiated (and the American was arguably the least libertarian of the three). And the gains by labor in this country were not negotiated; they were taken by force by people in the streets and the factories."

I agree with Thaler's reading of history. Sometimes political and legal systems fail. In some dire situations, public protests, including violent ones, have been the only tools that have moved institutions to respond. And in our era, marches, boycotts, sit-ins, and other public forms of protest have played important roles. Marches against the World Trade Organization, in Seattle and elsewhere, are an excellent recent example of how public protests can force changes when even legal action fails.

Others with more experience in this field have written about how to organize and lead public protests (see "Resources"). From what I've seen and heard as an activist, however, I offer this advice:

KEY POINT ■ *Think strategically when planning public protests. They are a means to an end; do not stage them in isolation. Public protests work best in concert with other means, such as negotiation, legislative action, and public education, that can take advantage of the openings created by the protests to forge positive, long-term gains.*

Slave trading was ended in Britain in the early 19th century, for example, not just by public protests, but also by a patient public relations campaign that led to a vote in Parliament. The civil rights movement in this country used carefully designed confrontations and lawsuits to increase pressure on Congress for new legislation. In the struggle for independence in India, Gandhi brilliantly used strikes and demonstrations to support his political initiatives for Indian independence—and the British left peacefully.

The primary purpose of public protests is *not* to create anarchy and chaos. The primary purpose is to force decision makers to pay attention to ideas they resist paying attention to, and then—when you've got their attention—to use the leverage you've created to bring about positive long-term change, using tools such as those detailed in this book. The more destructive and polarizing the protests are, however, and the more that violent emotions flare, the harder it becomes to seize or even to recognize the opportunities for settlement. Blood in the streets does not easily lead to reasoned discussions.

PLAY IT AGAIN

WHAT'S NEXT?
The epilogue offers some personal thoughts on active citizenship as a life's journey.

- *Prepare well for public testimony:*

  - *Know the ground rules for your hearing, understand the issues and the people, and make a plan.*

  - *Fill the room with "your" people.*

  - *Never assume that decision makers have the facts they need.*

- *Be as engaging and as positive as you can be:*

  - *Tell your story.*

  - *Keep the tone positive.*

  - *Be more open than you're comfortable with being.*

- *Don't overreach.*

- *Be prepared to take legal action when you have to, but know the downsides:*

  - *You could lose.*

  - *Legal action is conflict, impeding honest communication, making compromise difficult, and undermining opportunities for long-term solutions.*

  - *Your lawsuit may create enemies outside the courtroom.*

  - *Legal action lets everyone duck responsibilities they should be facing.*

- *In using legal action:*

  - *A good threat can be almost as powerful as the real thing.*

  - *Hire the right lawyer.*

  - *Don't wait too long to seek legal help.*

  - *Plan well.*

  - *Maintain control of your side's legal strategy.*

- Don't buy into the common perception of court proceedings as combat. Never burn your bridges behind you, because you never know what's coming next.

- Legal action should never be the only arrow in your quiver. At some point it's important to move the issues out of court and to establish working relationships with the people in the institutions that your legal action is seeking to shift.

- Your long-term goal should be more than a court order in your favor. Such an order is no substitute for long-term solutions that are stable because they are the result of honest talk and patient efforts to build common ground.

- Take advantage of the delays that the legal system provides. New information or new events during a protracted delay may present fresh opportunities for a negotiated settlement.

- Beyond legal action, public protests work best only in concert with other means—such as negotiation, legislative action, and public education—that can take advantage of the openings created by the protests to forge positive, long-term gains.

EPILOGUE

A PERSONAL JOURNEY

I KNOW FROM my own experience that it's not easy to stick your neck out, no matter how fervently you believe in your cause. I end this book with some personal reflections on how to deal with the challenges of active citizenship, emphasizing that these views are personal. I'm happy if you find value in them for your own activism and your own life.

To begin, my experience is that I am more successful as an active citizen if I set this work in the context of something bigger than myself. Call it God, higher power, life force—I find that being mindful of and connected to that larger reality adds to my power, creativity, commitment, and focus, especially when I'm under pressure. I'm talking about a spiritual view here, one that's not tied to any one religious faith.

The journey that has led me to explore and develop a spiritual life is not, I think, that unusual for someone my age: a balance of successes and failures, a good measure of mistakes and pain, some wise mentors and role models, more than a few hard kicks to the backside, and—to my credit—a willingness to learn.

Below, I share three thoughts from this journey that have a direct bearing on my work as an active citizen and, therefore, on the tone and substance of what you've read in this book. These thoughts focus on acknowledging connectedness, lightening up, and being responsible.

CONNECTEDNESS—A SPIRITUAL
CONCEPT WITH POLITICAL POWER

At the core of each of the world's great faiths is the same governing concept of unity: of each of us with each other and with the whole of creation. My picture of it is that we humans are not like balls on a billiard table, shoved this way and that to crash into each other and then slowly roll to a stop, alone. Instead we're connected to each other and to the rest of existence, at a point where mystics and quantum physicists have begun to converge. Meditators and atom smashers reaffirm this basic thought that we are all parts of a whole.

To me, the concept of connectedness is integral to creating political and social change.

How?

One way to see this linkage is to notice how many of the problems and challenges in the world today seem to come out of a perspective of *un*-connectedness—a mind-set that says indeed we *are* those billiard balls, left to fend for ourselves in a universe that is chaotic, impersonal, and threatening. Look at any conflicts today, in your household or in the world at large: see how much each of them flows from a perspective of separation, and how pain follows hard upon that. We see differences (for example, *your politics are different from mine*). We react to the differences with suspicion (*therefore you are strange*). Suspicion breeds fear (*what harm will you do me if your views prevail?*). Fear leads to alienation and judgments (*there's no way you and I can talk; you are stupid/evil/greedy* and so on). The judgments can lead to violence (*I'd better take you out before you take me out*).

What would it be like if, when we saw differences (an acting-out kid, a political opponent in the community, a foreigner full of rage against us), we considered, before our emotions spun us out of control, that the "opponent" was linked to us, not by some unsubstantiated theory or hope, but as a consequence of how the universe is in fact constructed? Such a perspective doesn't automatically change others. But I find that it at least slows down the rush to judgment, first in myself and then often in those I face. I find that it strengthens the search for common ground (chapter 7).

Another link between the experience of connectedness and active citizenship is in strengthening our power to care. I've said throughout this book that caring is vital to building trust and to creating positive, long-term change. But caring can be hard. What difference would it make if we acted on the premise that caring is not just an emotional response, not just a product of religious or parental training, not just a way to help us feel good? Those rationales for caring can be fragile, especially under fire. What if we saw instead that our caring flows from the very definition of who we are as connected parts of a whole?

In my experience, even *entertaining* the idea that I'm connected to the rest of creation deepens my caring and gives it more staying power, particularly when I'm dealing with difficult people and situations. Sure, I can let my fears overwhelm my caring, but if in my better moments I see my caring as a manifestation of something deeper, I'm far more likely to exercise it when things get tough. If the sharp-tongued neighbor, the unethical political opponent, the robber-baron CEO, and the Muslim teenager screaming obscenities at the United States are all part of me in some more-than-metaphorical way, then I'm led to invest more energy into trying to put myself in their shoes, into understanding the world the way they see it, even though I disagree with their actions. And this in turn makes it far more likely that I will see opportunities and avenues for solving problems that I might never have seen otherwise. I'm a better, more effective activist when I act from this understanding.

Still, this understanding of connectedness is so hard to put into practice in our daily lives that we are unlikely to do so unless we've had some personal experience of it. I think we all *do* have such experiences, if we just think about it. Reflect, for example, on why we stop to help a stranger.

I was once driving down a winding mountain road from a friend's house in Boulder, Colorado, when, coming around a curve, I saw a bicyclist sitting in the middle of the road, crying. She'd obviously taken a fall from her bike. Of course I stopped and helped her to the side of the road. It turned out she had only some bruises. But if I'd had to take her to a hospital, I certainly would have done that, and been late—or missed—my meeting. And I would have done it as a matter of course.

My point is not that I did this or that you would have done it. My point is that almost *anybody* would have done it. To me, a "Good Samaritan" act is rarely a rational act but almost always an *instinctive* one. The only explanation that makes sense to me is that this behavior reflects an innate connectedness hardwired into us. If jumping back from a loud noise stems from a primeval instinct of self-preservation, then why can't the impulse to help someone in need stem from an equally basic instinct that that person is in some real way a part of us? Sure, this instinct can be overwhelmed and buried in many of us, but I see it there nonetheless, even in people who in every other way seem to be villains. That's why, at least initially, I always give my opponents the benefit of the doubt and try to establish some trust with them. That's also why they so often take the same risk with me in return (see "Building Trust Is Often the Key to Success" in chapter 7, page 98).

WHAT'S YOUR EXPERIENCE? ■ *Think of the last time you went out of your way to help a stranger. Did you think it through before acting? Or did you just do it?*

KEY POINT ■ *Acknowledging connectedness as an innate part of the human condition is the soundest basis I know for building a more connected world and for understanding how each of us might act in it.*

LIGHTENING UP

Lightening up is a simple lesson that has taken me a lifetime to learn. I grew up filtering everything through my head and not my heart. As a Foreign Service Officer, and then in my first years as a political activist, I led with my mind. I saw all the serious problems in the world and thought I had to be "serious" about solving them. I did rigorous homework. I wrote out detailed speeches and workshop outlines. Then I wondered when I saw people nodding in agreement at the things I was saying but not being inspired to take the actions I was suggesting.

I had the facts. But in communicating them I was coming across like a Puritan preacher. I described citizen activism as a duty, not as an opportunity. In trying to be absolutely open to people about the risks of taking political action, I made everything sound grim and tough.

I credit my wife, Ann, with helping me turn this around. In starting the Giraffe Heroes Project, she saw the same public problems that I did, and she knew, as I did, how tough they were. But the

Project she designed had outrageous giraffe imagery, and the tone she used in telling Giraffe stories was joyful, irreverent, and—dare I say it—funny. People flocked to the Giraffe Heroes Project as much as they avoided my "serious" seminars. They would smile at the imagery and the tone. Relaxed and comfortable, they could then absorb the "stick your neck out" message behind the Giraffe stories without feeling guilty or fearful. And many have been motivated to take action.

So one impetus for me to lighten up was very practical. Ann and I were both trying to change people's behavior, but I could see directly from her work how much better a lighter approach worked.

The strongest push for me to lighten up, however, was the development of a spiritual life and, as a consequence, an acknowledgment that I was not alone. I stopped seeing the world with its problems as resting on my shoulders alone. I increasingly saw myself and my work in the context of something bigger than both. I still took the political issues I was dealing with seriously, but I lightened up about myself. The pressure off, I learned to laugh at my mistakes. I told stories. I became more spontaneous. *Joy became part of my life, and therefore part of my communications with others.*

Four things happened almost immediately: my audiences responded much more positively; my stress levels dropped; my energy soared; and, in my own efforts as an activist, I became more credible, more persuasive, and better able to build trust.

KEY POINT ■ *In my experience, joy smooths the way for creativity and power. It is the grease, the lubricant, that allows the power of the universe to flow. In words usually attributed to Teilhard de Chardin, "Joy is the infallible sign of the presence of God."*

Now a convert, I speak often on the importance of lightening up and the power of joy. Recently I was to give a speech on these themes at a conference in Switzerland to people who were intensely involved in conflicts in their home countries. Many of them would return home to war and famine and disease. Knowing the audience I would face, Ann e-mailed me the night before the speech, warning me, in her inimitable way, not to come across as naive to this audience of battle-hardened activists.

I told the audience that I was not suggesting they ignore the dismal facts of their conflicts, or the pain, or the need to grieve.

But I also said what I am now saying to you. From my experience, if you burden your work with sadness and frustration, it becomes much harder. You risk burning out. You risk missing opportunities. The challenge is to take difficult work very seriously, but to reflect an essential lightness at the core of your being. No one at that conference, as far as I know, took these thoughts to be naive.

BEING RESPONSIBLE FOR OUR WORLD—AND FOR OURSELVES

Yes, we need to take responsibility for solving the problems that test us in our communities and in the world. Humanity—and your community—can improve its future only if more people put their hearts and heads to work. The task is huge, not just because the problems today are huge, but also because we face an epidemic of irresponsibility.

I've no doubt that there are leaders of large pharmaceutical firms who act with compassion in their own families and communities at the same time as they deny life-saving drugs to AIDS victims in Africa who cannot afford them, blaming "market forces" for their actions.

The corporate scammers of 2003–4 did what they did, not just because they thought they could get away with it, but because, at their level in the jungle, they considered it the norm. "Everybody else was doing it, so why not?"

The bigger the arena, the more places there are for people to hide and the easier it is for people to be irresponsible. War is perhaps the ultimate expression of irresponsibility. War makers justify their actions on the basis of security and politics, and I'm not saying these justifications are always false. But I've been in violent situations from Libya to Vietnam, and from the inside I can tell you that what starts most conflicts, and certainly what keeps all of them going, is the failure of individuals—leaders and those who support them—to take responsibility for their own fear, rage, and ignorance. War provides a seal of approval for organized violence that is permitted nowhere else. War too often allows individuals to act out with weapons the personal failings they refuse to deal with in any other way.

Irresponsibility filters downward. We see what Enron did and we feel not so guilty about cheating on our own tax returns. My personal peeve is sports and the images that some athletes project.

What does it say to viewers when a baseball player waves the ball above his head, trying to fool the umpire into believing that he caught it, when he knows, and the instant replay shows, that he didn't? "Just part of the game," the announcer says, approvingly.

I think the challenge for each one of us is to help turn this bigger "game" around. We can fight to change irresponsible policies and reverse irresponsible actions. We can call leaders to account. But—

KEY POINT ■ *Irresponsibility is a mind-set, and nothing will really improve until the mind-set changes—until more people accept that the fate of ourselves and of our communities and of the world is up to us.*

We can promote that change by visibly being more responsible in our personal lives, becoming role models, both for those who make irresponsible policies and for those who ignore the good policies we have. We can, through our responsible actions, also be models to those who pass the buck and those who believe that "someone else" is always responsible for what goes wrong. We can influence those who think that what they do or don't do doesn't really matter, or that nobody will notice, or that someone else, maybe some government agency, will pick up the pieces.

■ Attitudes Count Too

Here comes the hard part. In my view, what's needed are not only models of responsible words and actions, but models of responsible *attitudes* as well.

Why? Because I think all of us are constantly shaping our workplaces, our homes, our communities, and even our world, not just by our words and actions, but also by our attitudes.

Think about times when you or someone else in your family comes home after a very bad day or a very good one; the evening for the entire family can be affected by that one person's attitude. Notice the power of one person to set the mood for an entire workplace.

We've all had the experience of being endangered by somebody else's driving mistakes. Somebody cuts in front of us or fails to look both ways and we jam on the brakes, narrowly avoiding a collision. We honk our horn, and in the confines of our car we rant. "Did you see what that guy did?" "What a stupid jerk!" "Idiot!" Our blood is still hot when we park the car and head into the meeting with our kid's teacher, our business colleagues, or the city council. Unless we've taken steps to calm down, our anger will affect that meeting, especially if we extend the rant toward the people around us.

WHAT'S YOUR EXPERIENCE? ■ *Recall a situation in which the attitude of just one person changed the mood of an entire group. Have you ever been that person?*

■ You Don't Have to See It to Believe It

Many times you might think your actions or attitudes are too minor to affect anything, or that nobody will notice. My experience is that you can't know. Just because you can't see the effects of your actions or attitudes doesn't mean they aren't real. You can influence others by your example and never see or hear about it.

CASE STUDY At the United Nations

In chapters 1 and 3, I told the story of how I played a role in getting the United Nations to enforce a tougher arms embargo on the apartheid regime in South Africa. No, the half dozen or so of us who took the risks to pull this off didn't change the world. But plenty of other people at the UN and at foreign ministries around the world learned of what we did, and I can't help thinking we inspired some of them to similar behavior on some problem they were facing. I think there was a legacy to our actions that went beyond the embargo itself, even if we never heard about it.

KEY POINT ■ *Both our behavior and our attitudes affect the people and events around us, whether or not we see or hear about it. In my view, then, it just makes sense for us to be more conscious of both so that we can play a greater role in shaping the outcomes.*

■ No One Said It Was Easy

Yes, it's tough to be responsible in this more comprehensive way. And none of us, certainly including me, does it right every time. But here's a suggestion:

TRY THIS ■ *Look at any situation you're in as if it were a stage play, with yourself as one of the actors, and with much of the audience beyond the reach of the stage lights, out of your sight.*

Consider that every one of your actions and attitudes helps write the script for that play, whether or not you see it and whether or not you like it. If what you contribute to the script are anger, blame, cynicism, fear, or hopelessness—and if your actions are motivated by attitudes like these—then you push the final act of the play in that direction.

On the other hand, if the behavior and attitudes you bring to that situation are caring, courageous, and hopeful, you'll influence events in that direction.

CASE STUDY **Island County**

As the leader of the Citizens' Coalition, I testified often at the county seat on contentious land-use issues. I faced opponents from many quarters, and many of them were so rude and insulting that I found it very hard to keep my cool. Early on, therefore, I said to myself, OK, I'm only human; I'll allow myself two lapses a year when I can blow up, return insult with insult, and/or stomp out of the room.

The problem was, I used up those two free passes in the first month. So I struggled to follow my own advice in this book, to stay calm and caring under pressure. When that first year ended and I realized that I had done well for 11 months, there came an epiphany: Why should I give myself any free passes at all? If I can stay calm and focused under fire for 11 months, I can do it for an entire year—or two. It was like cutting down on coffee. The challenge seemed hard at first, but after I established a rhythm and a track record, it got easier.

Think of an upcoming meeting in which you have to deal with people who think differently than you do and who perhaps make you uncomfortable. I'm suggesting that you'll do a much better job at the meeting if you check your attitudes before it starts, so that you can take responsibility for them as well as for your behavior—and try to change both if they're negative.

Are you dragging in any emotional baggage, any prejudices or old grudges? Are you upset or angry from something totally unrelated to that meeting, such as a fight with a friend that morning? Will that baggage interfere with your acting responsibly in this situation? Will it pop out in your body language? Will it undercut your power or your good judgment?

If you take responsibility and dump that baggage, you'll be better able to focus cleanly on what needs to be done and said at the meeting.

It's just as important, in my view, to take responsibility for positive behavior and attitudes. At that difficult meeting, for example, taking responsibility could mean cooling a conflict with your good humor, bringing up a difficult subject with respect and sensitivity, or offering a caring word or gesture to someone who's hurting.

Defining and accepting responsibility in this way is a tough thing to do because it means you're constantly "on duty," accepting that even something you might think is a minor act or a momentary attitude can have effects that go beyond your own life. It also means accepting that you can inspire others to their best behavior through your best behavior and, in doing so, decisively improve what happens.

▪ Take It from Me—It's Worth It

I'm suggesting that it makes sense to at least try to take responsibility in this more comprehensive way, no matter how difficult. It will make you more effective as an agent of change—clearer, more focused, and more effective.

It will also give you more authority.

I've never forgotten one dispirited staff meeting in Vietnam. The discussion among the senior officers was going nowhere until a gutsy second lieutenant said to the general who was chairing the meeting, "Sir, I've got an idea." Every head turned, everyone listened to that idea, and a version of it was adopted. The lieutenant had taken responsibility for his idea and, as a consequence, had been given authority by a group of men all senior to him in rank.

KEY POINT ■ *What I learned from this incident was that by taking responsibility—by filling a vacuum of inaction with action—you receive the authority that action brings.*

The bottom line to me from all this is that our every action and every attitude can make a difference. When we realize this, and act on it, we can change relationships, organizations, communities— and beyond. In taking responsibility in this deeper way, we become not just agents of change but role models—people who can move others, including our leaders, to act responsibly, too. Working to change policies and conditions we don't like can produce important victories, but if we also consciously try to model what it means to be fully responsible, we can change the world.

I find that being responsible in this way is also an immensely rich and powerful opportunity for living life to the fullest. Again, poet Mary Oliver's question: "Tell me, what is it you plan to do with your one wild and precious life?"

I hope your plan is to make your one wild and precious life as important as it is meant to be.

God bless.

■ Chapter 1—Why Do It?

Csikszentmihalyi, Mihaly. *Flow: The Psychology of Optimal Experience.*
London: Harper Perennial, 1990. See especially chapter 10, on
the making of meaning.

Frankl, Viktor E. *Man's Search for Meaning.* Rev. and updated ed.
New York: Washington Square Press, 1985. A classic with relevance for active citizenship today.

■ Chapter 2—Start Here

Ames, Steven C. *Guide to Community Visioning: Hands-On Information
for Local Communities.* Rev. ed. Chicago: APA Planners Press,
1998. This book helps citizens understand the connection
between the kind of place they want their community to be
and the policies that will support their vision. It shows how to
design and implement an effective visioning process.

The Center for Rural Pennsylvania. *Planning for the Future: A
Handbook on Community Visioning.* 2nd ed. Harrisburg, PA: The
Center for Rural Pennsylvania, 717-787-9555. The focus of this
guide is on defining and creating vision, elements of successful visioning, and helpful case studies.

■ Chapter 3—Trust *Them?* Are You Kidding?

Bracey, Hyler. *Building Trust: How to Get It! How to Keep It!*
Taylorsville, GA: HB Artworks, 2003. A practical, helpful book.

Solomon, Robert C., and Fernando Flores. *Building Trust: In Business,
Politics, Relationships, and Life.* New York: Oxford University
Press, 2003. The authors assert that trust is an emotional skill,
an active and dynamic part of our lives that we build and sustain with our promises and commitments, our emotions and
integrity.

■ Chapter 4—Building a Team and Keeping It Together

Hawkins, Charlie. *First Aid for Meetings: Quick Fixes and Major Repairs
for Running Effective Meetings.* Wilsonville, OR: Bookpartners, 1997.
Provides strategies, tips, and tools for improving the planning
and effectiveness of meetings.

Hummel, Joan M. *Starting and Running a Nonprofit Organization.* 2nd
ed. Minneapolis: University of Minnesota Press, 1996. A standard handbook that describes, step-by-step, all of the phases of
creating and operating a new nonprofit organization, including
obtaining tax-exempt status and creating a strategic plan.

Katzenbach, Jon R., and Douglas Smith. *The Wisdom of Teams:
Creating the High-Performance Organization.* New York: Harper
Business Essentials, 2003. The authors distinguish between
true teams and leader-led work groups.

Scholtes, Peter R., Brian L. Joiner, and Barbara J. Streibel. *The
Team Handbook, Third Edition.* Madison, WI: Oriel Inc., 2003. An
easy-to-use, comprehensive reference book useful to anyone
involved with teams.

Schwarz, Roger M. *The Skilled Facilitator: Practical Wisdom for Developing
Effective Groups.* San Francisco: Jossey-Bass, 1994. This is a basic
organization-development text, and, while a bit dry, it has
many useful suggestions for making groups more effective.

■ Chapter 5—Making a Plan

Allison, Michael, and Jude Kaye. *Strategic Planning for Nonprofit Organizations: A Practical Guide and Workbook*. 2nd ed. Hoboken, NJ: John Wiley & Sons, 2005. This accessible resource from a team of experts in the nonprofit sector adapts basic business concepts to the unique structure and goals of nonprofit organizations.

Fogg, C. Davis. *Team-Based Strategic Planning: A Complete Guide to Structuring, Facilitating and Implementing the Process*. New York: American Management Association, 1994. Provides a useful framework for engaging a wide range of individuals in the planning process.

■ Chapter 6—Risk Taking and Courage

Osho. *Courage: The Joy of Living Dangerously*. New York: St. Martin's Griffin, 1999. Provides a bird's-eye view of the whole terrain: where fears originate, how to understand them, and how to find the courage to face them.

Treasurer, Bill. *Right Risk: 10 Powerful Principles for Taking Giant Leaps with Your Life*. San Francisco: Berrett-Koehler, 2003. The author draws on the experiences and insights of 10 successful risk takers to detail 10 principles for taking risks with greater intelligence and confidence.

■ Chapter 7—Finding Common Ground: Negotiating and Resolving Conflicts

Levine, Stewart. *Getting to Resolution: Turning Conflict into Collaboration*. San Francisco: Berrett-Koehler, 2000. Levine's seven-step model integrates two skills essential for success— collaboration and conflict resolution—and emphasizes the importance of a shift in attitude, assumptions, and approaches when facing a problem.

Straus, David. *How to Make Collaboration Work: Powerful Ways to Build Consensus, Solve Problems, and Make Decisions*. San Francisco: Berrett-Koehler, 2002. This work discusses why collaborative problem solving seems so hard and describes five useful principles for making collaborative efforts more joyful.

Ury, William. *Getting Past No: Negotiating Your Way from Confrontation to Cooperation*. Rev. ed. New York: Bantam, 1993. A very practical, easy-to-read guide and process.

▪ Chapter 8—Persuasive Communications: Speeches, Fund-Raising, and More

Detz, Joan. *It's Not What You Say, It's How You Say It: Ready-to-Use Advice for Presentations, Speeches, and Other Speaking Occasions, Large and Small*. New York: St. Martin's Griffin, 2000. A useful and lively book presenting strategies and tips for speeches, brief remarks, Q & A sessions, panels, and more—every situation that requires something to say.

The Foundation Center. *The Foundation Directory Online*. http://fconline.fdncenter.org. A good fee-based directory of foundations.

Garecht, Joe, and Brent Barksdale. *25 Fundraising Secrets*. Instantpublisher.Com, 2002. Tested strategies that can help you raise money.

Robinson, Andy. *Selling Social Change (Without Selling Out)*. San Francisco: Chardon Press Series, Jossey-Bass, 2002. Good book on earned-income strategies for nonprofits.

Stallings, Betty, and Donna McMillion. *How to Produce Fabulous Fundraising Events: Reap Remarkable Returns with Minimal Effort*. Book & Diskette ed. Building Better Skills, 1999. Practical tips and tools.

Warwick, Mal. *How to Write Successful Fundraising Letters*. San Francisco: Jossey-Bass, 2001. Warwick offers detailed advice and analysis along with copious examples and instructive case studies.

▪ Chapter 9—Dealing with the Media:
The Secrets of Good PR

Andreasen, Alan R. *Marketing Social Change: Changing Behavior to Promote Health, Social Development, and the Environment.* San Francisco: Jossey-Bass, 1995. This book applies commercial marketing technology to nonprofit social-change efforts.

Bonk, Kathy, Henry Griggs, and Emily Tynes. *The Jossey-Bass Guide to Strategic Communications for Nonprofits: A Step-by-Step Guide to Working with the Media to Generate Publicity, Enhance Fundraising, Build Membership, Change Public Policy, Handle Crises, and More!* San Francisco: Jossey-Bass, 1999. Excellent techniques and useful tools in a practical guide for social-change agents.

Crowder, David A., and Rhonda Crowder. *Building a Web Site for Dummies.* Book and CD-ROM ed. For Dummies, 2000. Includes navigation principles, affiliation possibilities, building communications with your users, and other wide-ranging topics.

Sweeney, Susan. *101 Ways to Promote Your Web Site: Filled with Proven Internet Marketing Tips, Tools, Techniques, and Resources to Increase Your Web Site Traffic.* Gulf Breeze, FL: Maximum Press, 2003. This guide provides tools such as templates, checklists, and forms, as well as proven techniques such as using e-mail, links, and online advertising to increase the number of initial users and repeat visitors to a Web site.

▪ Chapter 10—Getting Institutions to Do What You Want

Barone, Michael, with Richard E. Cohen. *The Almanac of American Politics.* Washington, D.C.: National Journal Group, 2004. Contains profiles of every governor and member of Congress, as well as economic, social, historical, and political background information about all 50 states and 435 House of Representatives districts.

Mathews, David, and Noelle McAfee. *Community Politics,* 2nd ed. Dayton, Ohio: Kettering Foundation, 1993. An excellent book on how to identify and build public will.

Contacting the Congress: Online Directory for the 108th U.S. Congress.
www.visi.com/juan/congress.

■ Chapter 11—Public Testimony and Legal Action

Beaudry, Ann, and Bob Schaeffer. *Winning Local and State Elections: The Guide to Organizing Your Campaign.* New York: Free Press, 1998. A direct, very basic guide to running a political campaign.

Friedman, Monroe. *Consumer Boycotts: Effecting Change Through the Marketplace and the Media.* New York: Routledge, 1999. Friedman discusses different types of boycotts, from their historical focus on labor and economic concerns to the more recent inclusion of issues such as minority rights and environmental protection.

Jasper, James M. *The Art of Moral Protest: Culture, Biography, and Creativity in Social Movements.* Chicago: University of Chicago Press, 1999. Jasper emphasizes four dimensions of protest: culture, resources, strategies, and biographies.

Matthews, Joseph L. *The Lawsuit Survival Guide: A Client's Companion to Litigation.* Berkeley: Nolo, 2001. This book helps demystify the lawsuit process and encourages clients' informed participation and decision making.

Powers, Roger S., William B. Vogele, Christopher Kruegler, and Ronald M. McCarthy. *Protest, Power, and Change: An Encyclopedia of Nonviolent Action from ACT-UP to Women's Suffrage.* New York: Garland Publishing, 1997. A systematic survey of peaceful confrontations between the forces of the status quo and the forces for change.

Thomas, Robert J., and Doug Gowen. *How to Run for Local Office: A Complete Guide for Winning a Local Election.* R & T Enterprises, Inc., 1999. While this book was written with the first-time candidate in mind, it's a good resource for anyone running for office.

ABOUT THE AUTHOR

John Graham shipped out on a freighter when he was 16, took part in the first ascent of Mt. McKinley's North Wall at 20, and hitch-hiked around the world at 22.

A Foreign Service Officer for 15 years, he was in the middle of the revolution in Libya and the war in Vietnam. For three years in the mid-1970s he was a member of NATO's top-secret Nuclear Planning Group, then served as a foreign-policy adviser to Senator John Glenn. As an assistant to Ambassador Andrew Young at the United Nations, he was deeply involved in U.S. initiatives in southern Africa, South Asia, and Cuba. By most measures he was very successful.

But something was missing.

In 1980, a close brush with death aboard a burning cruise ship in the North Pacific forced him to a deeper search for how he could put his ideals for a better world into action. He found the perfect vehicle in the Giraffe Heroes Project, an international organization that inspires people to stick their necks out for the common good and gives them tools to succeed. He's been a leader of the Project since 1983.

Learning from the courageous men and women honored by the Project, and from his own life experiences, Graham has for the last 20 years been teaching people how to stick their necks out to help solve public problems in their communities and beyond. Now he's put what he knows into this book.

A familiar keynote speaker, Graham talks on themes of risk taking, meaning, and service at national and regional conferences of all kinds, and to companies, service organizations, advocacy groups, universities, schools, churches, government agencies, trade unions, leadership groups, and outdoor clubs. His interactive workshops help people to deal with conflicts, and to create and communicate visions for success that inspire others and attract resources.

Graham walks his talk: in the 1990s he was a leader of an environmental coalition in the Pacific Northwest, where he lives, and now he is an international peacemaker, active in the Middle East and Africa.

Graham has done TV and radio all over the world. Articles about him have appeared in major magazines and newspapers. Previous books include *Outdoor Leadership: Technique, Common Sense & Self-Confidence* (Seattle: Mountaineers Books, 1997) and *It's Up to Us* (Langley, WA: Giraffe Heroes Project, 1999).

He has a bachelor's degree in geology from Harvard University and a master's degree in engineering from Stanford University, neither of which he ever expects to use.

RESOURCES

213

INDEX

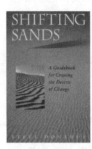

Berrett-Koehler books are available at quantity discounts for orders of 10 or more copies.

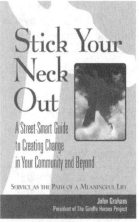

Stick Your Neck Out

John Graham

Paperback original, 312 pages
ISBN 978-1-57675-304-0
Item# 93040 $14.95

To find out about discounts for orders of 10 or more copies for individuals, corporations, institutions, and organizations, please call us toll-free at (800) 929-2929.

To find out about our discount programs for resellers, please contact our Special Sales department at (415) 288-0260; Fax: (415) 362-2512.
Or email us at bkpub@bkpub.com.

Subscribe to our free e-newsletter!

To find out about what's happening at Berrett-Koehler and to receive announcements of our new books, special offers, free excerpts, and much more, subscribe to our free monthly e-newsletter at www.bkconnection.com.

Berrett-Koehler Publishers
PO Box 565, Williston, VT 05495-9900
Call toll-free! **800-929-2929** 7 am-9 pm EST

Or fax your order to 1-802-864-7626
For fastest service order online: **www.bkconnection.com**